FIRST PRINTING
MARCH 1942
of

THE BACHELOR in NEW ORLEANS

by
ROBERT KINNEY

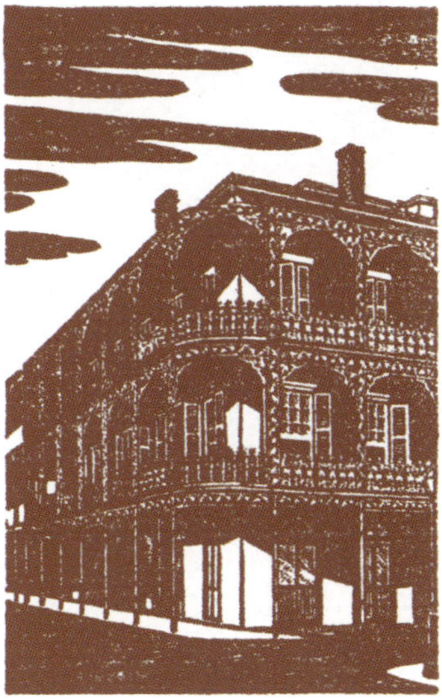

PUBLISHED BY
BOB RILEY STUDIOS INC.

THE BACHELOR IN NEW ORLEANS

A handbook for unattached gentlemen and ladies of spirit visiting or resident in the Paris of America

by

ROBERT KINNEY

illustrated
with hand block prints
by

Eugenia and Bob Riley

Reprinted by
Garrett County Press

Restored by Kevin Stone

Printed in Lithuania

Nostalgically
dedicated
to
THE OLD BUNCH
Bob and Mammy
Boo and Jane
Morrey and Pat
Warren
Jack and Helen
Wild Quill
Phil and Ginny
Al, Kelsey, A. G.
and the rest

Who'd never
turn down a glass—
with anything in it.

FOREWORD

This is not strictly a guidebook. Don't expect in these pages to come upon the information someone s h o u t s through a megaphone from the front of a sightseeing bus. This book is not for those who would be led.

This little book is, say, a handbook for those not afraid to find out for themselves.

★ ★ ★ ★ ★

CONTENTS

★ ★ ★ ★ ★

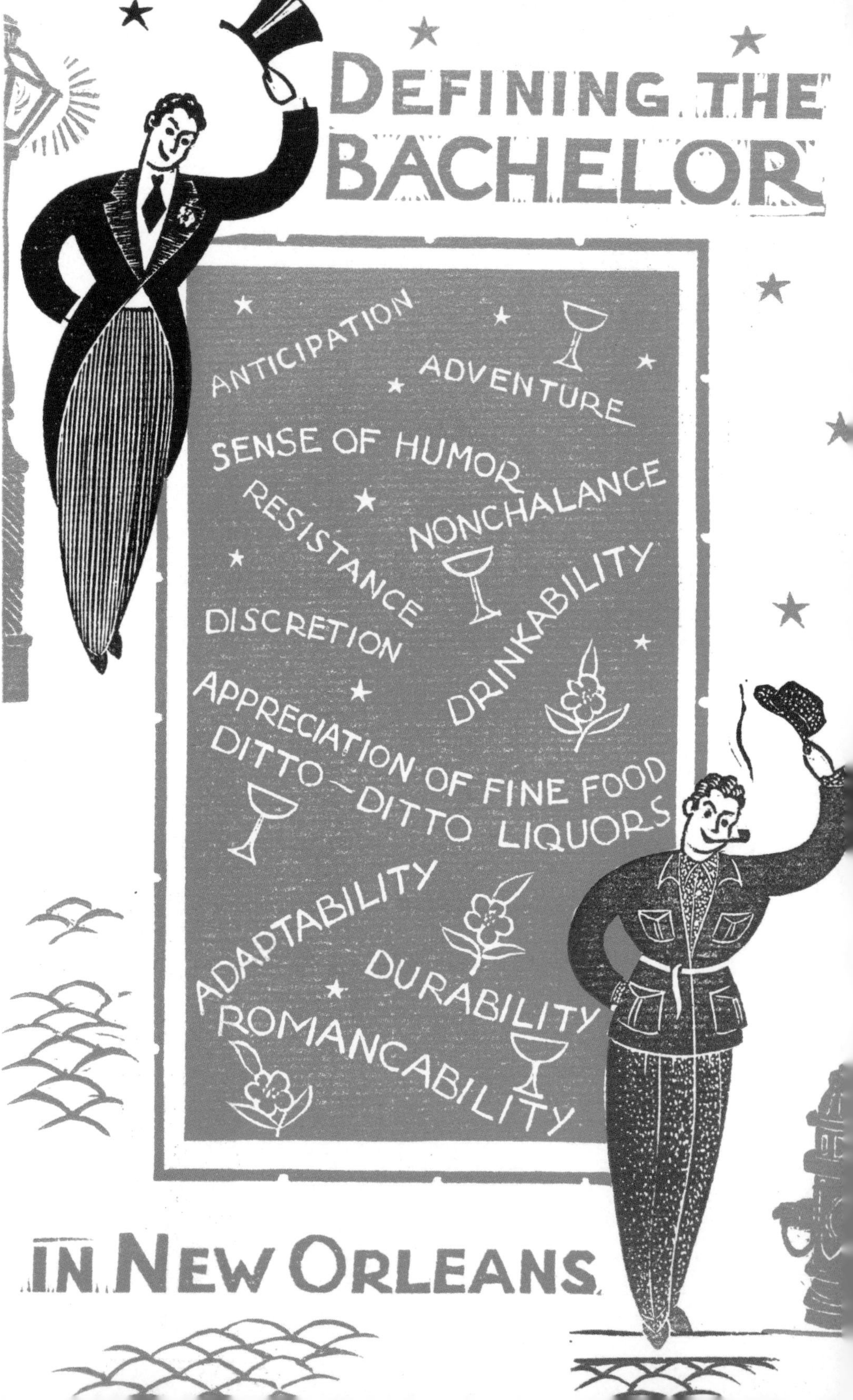
DEFINING THE BACHELOR
ANTICIPATION
ADVENTURE
SENSE OF HUMOR
RESISTANCE
NONCHALANCE
DISCRETION
DRINKABILITY
APPRECIATION OF FINE FOOD
DITTO – DITTO LIQUORS
ADAPTABILITY
DURABILITY
ROMANCABILITY
IN NEW ORLEANS

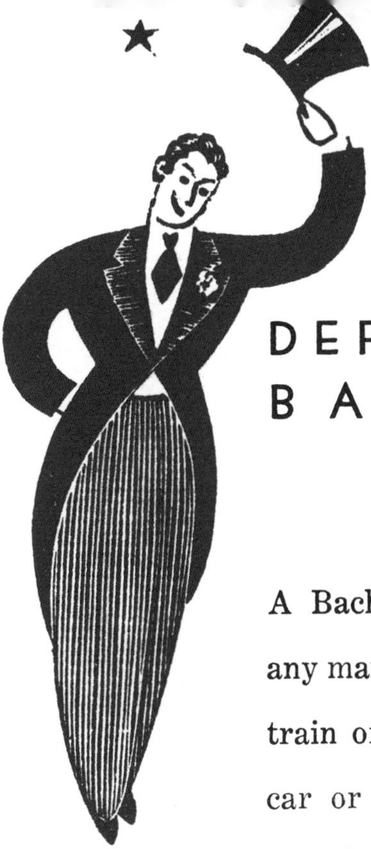

DEFINING THE BACHELOR

PREFACE

A Bachelor in **New Orleans** is any man or woman who gets off a train or bus or plane or out of a car or wheel-chair alone and unguarded, minus wife, husband, mother-in-law or detective to watch him or her while here.

A male Bachelor in New Orleans is the man you meet in Pat O'Bricn's one night at nine, at Cafe Lafitte the next morning at six, in Tony Bacino's Bar that afternoon at five and in the next cell the next day at ten. (You'll meet

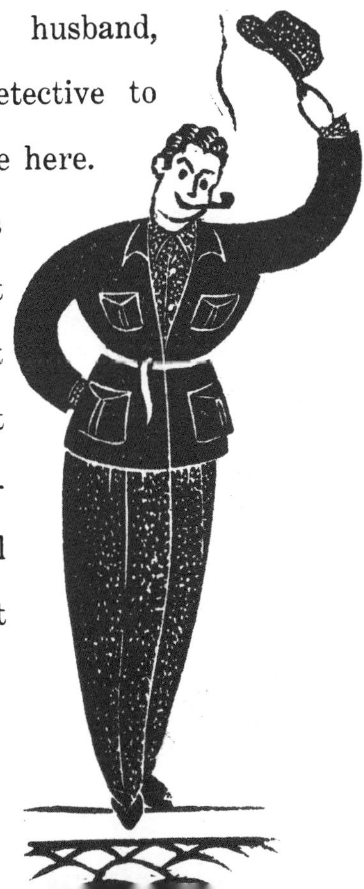

him in between times, too, but where you'll never tell anyone except another Bachelor in New Orleans!)

A Bachelor in New Orleans is a brave, lordly creature at night, a gay prowler on exciting missions; yet in the morning this party is a shambling furry creature who says *baaaaaa* disconsolately at the heavens.

A male Bachelor in New Orleans is the fellow you asked up for a drink five years ago, and who now lives in most of your apartment while you and your wife sleep in the kitchen sink.

A Bacheloress (pardon) in New Orleans is the girl five hundred Bachelors somewhere are worried about. She sends them postcards of night-life scenes.

A male Bachelor in New Orleans is the

guy who one night put a beautiful passed-out blonde in your bed so you wouldn't feel lonesome when you woke up to find that he'd left for San Francisco wearing your best suit and carrying all but one of your best shirts in your best suitcase.

A Bachelor in New Orleans is the man or woman who has a past that finds it difficult to keep up with his or her present.

A Bachelor in New Orleans, in short, is the person who is out for one hell of a good time and who is sure to find it. This Bachelor is never the one who peeks through anybody's latticework or grill: this Bachelor is the one who is peeked *at*! . . . .

By now, Bachelors in New Orleans, you should know who you are—so let's take a look at your town and what she has to offer.

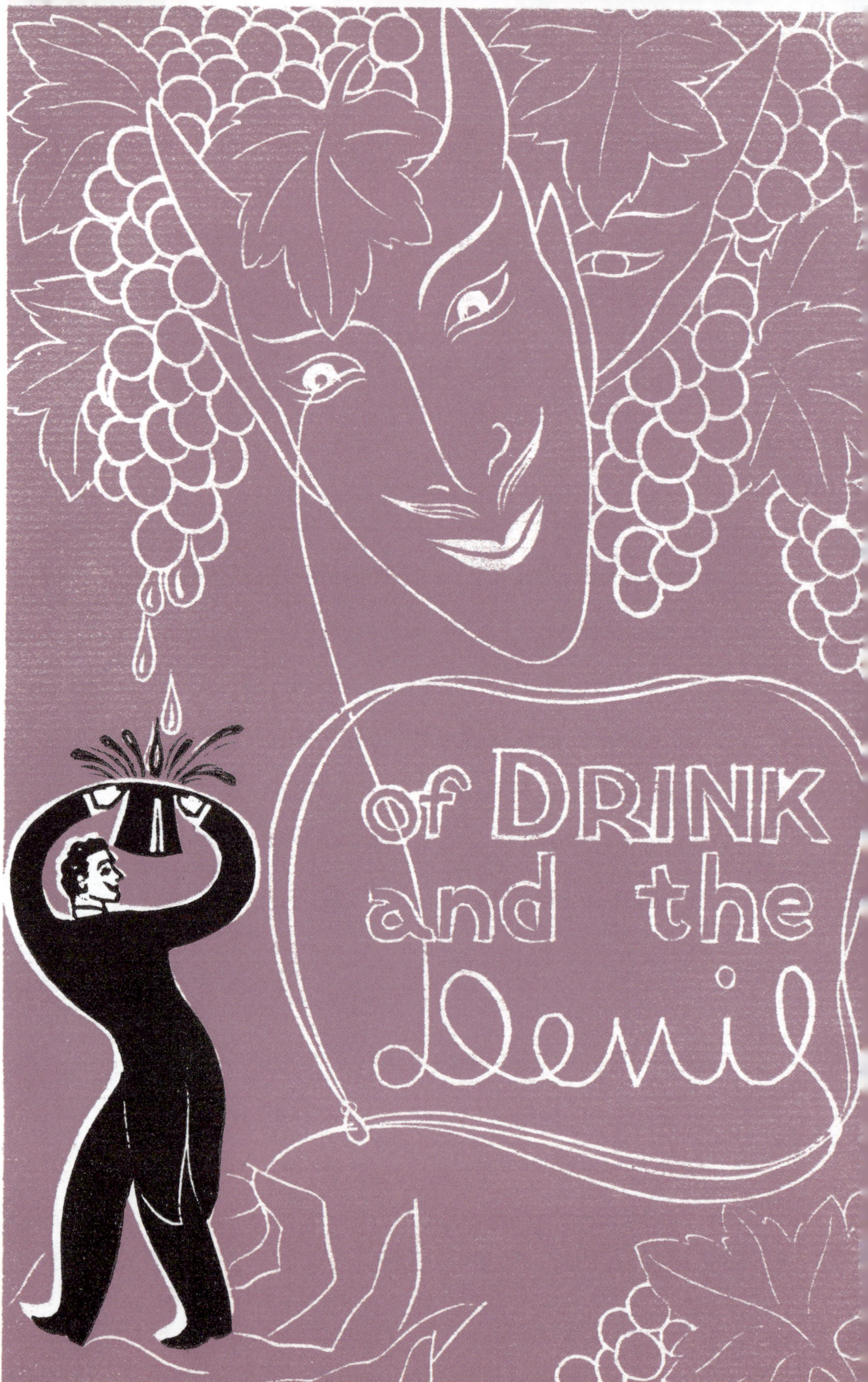
of DRINK
and the
Devil

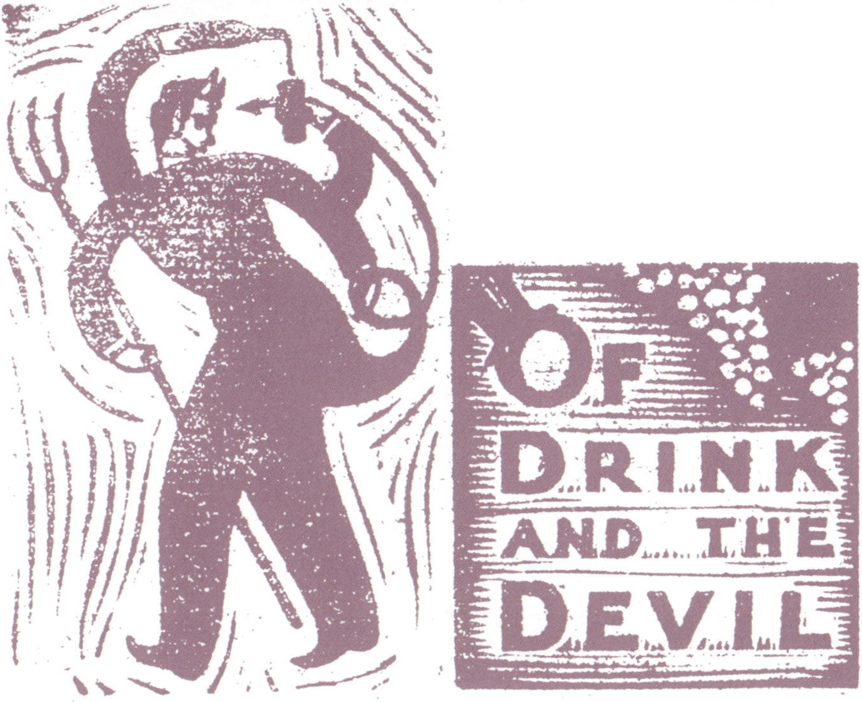

CHAPTER ONE

Few Bachelors in New Orleans really know whether New Orleans is an alcoholic mirage or whether New Orleans drinks are part of a general illusion, including wrought-iron grillwork, impossibly beautiful women, magnolia blossoms, race horses, carnival parades and Mardi Gras, moonlight, and the suggestive music seeping out into the streets from a hundred courtyards.

When—if ever—you leave New Orleans for that place you used to call home, and sober up or wake up or just generally get back to your old dull, sick, unpleasant normal self, you never know about this. You only know it was swell, whether it was the drinks that created the city or the city that created the drinks.

But still, that drinks exist in New Orleans, drinks that never taste the same anywhere else, is not merely a rumor. Wondrous drinks there are, and in great quantity.

Now, the drinks of New Orleans come in a number of varieties, sizes, shapes, and smells. Some are young little drinks, hoping to grow up some day and be president. And some are of draft age, nice, healthy, red blooded fellows with muscle to 'em. Some are married, with children. And some are elderly dignified chaps, mellow and courteous, but still good for a night of it with the boys, if need be, still with lead in their pencils. We shall consider a few representative ones, in turn . . . . .

Among the lustiest if not quite the youngest of the adolescent drinks—sure to become at least a senator on the independent ticket when he's old enough—is the brilliant-hued long, tall boy whose mama had him in the West Indies, the Zombie! Now, the Zombie can be found yowling for attention in almost any bar hereabouts, from the large Roosevelt to the small Bourbon House. You can recognize him not only by his terrific kick—one of the rums in his veins is 151 proof!—but by the violent red of his diapers. He is a dangerous brat, this Zombie. Even you doughty Bachelors in New Orleans should hesitate before placing this lad in your laps more than twice at one sitting. (It is an advertised rule of most bars that no one customer shall be served more than two Zombies, but the Bachelor in New Orleans should have not too much difficulty in persuading his bartender to serve him a third if he is so courageous *and* if he is able to keep his perch on his chair or stool while ordering.)

Another notable youngster, sure to please, at least, in any running of the bar derby, is the quiet-voiced and polite *but* potent Cafe Lafitte Special. This fellow is native to the shakers of Cafe Lafitte, as his name implies. There are applejack and curacao, among other nice things, in the blood of this comer.

Many are the New Orleans drink specialties tried and true and old enough to have been drafted into the national army. First, of course, is the handsome red Sazerac, a smooth-voiced guy with a terrific right and a wicked left, to boot. He comes dressed in an old-fashioned glass. Bourbon (pronounced *burbun,* suh!) whiskey, Peychaud and Angostura bitters, and a whiff of absinthe[1] combine to make him a fine friend but one hell of a guy with whom to go to the ropes. He can be found lounging in any bar in town, but big Joe Guerrera makes a perfect beauty of him at his Hotel Senator Bar.

And then there's that fancy-pants of a tall drink, the famous Ramos Gin Fizz. The Ramos can't be described simply. He's a boul-

[1]Imitation absinthe is always used, as the laws of most countries prohibit manufacture of the genuine liquor.

vardier, a gallant, a lady-killer, and a handsome Dan, all mixed to form the ne plus ultra in fancy gin drinks. The Roosevelt Bar owns the copyright to his formula and makes a specialty of him.

One of the older fellows, but a *very* dangerous guy if you hit him too hard, is the Absinthe Drip, a cloudy green gentleman popular all over the continent of Europe in the good old days before teetotalling Adolphe and a favorite of New Orleans Bachelors for more than a century. So well received is the Absinthe Drip that he is to be found in almost any New Orleans bar. The time-hallowed Old Absinthe House Bar—at one time, it is said, the rendezvous of pirate-soldier Jean Lafitte and his men—makes a specialty of the drink. Incidentally, the Absinthe Drip makes a very fine pick-up if you're feeling uncertain in the morning—*and* if you've no complicated tasks to perform for a few days.

Cafe brulot is an oldster that may not be overlooked, either. Not strictly a bar drink, *Cafe brulot* is best ordered in one of the better

New Orleans restaurants. It consists of flaming brandy mixed with coffee, and once sampled, is unforgettable. A fancy relation of this after-dinner drink is *Cafe diabolo*, which is rather much the same thing but is served in a cup made of orange peel, adding piquancy.

These are just a few of the more outstanding local favorites, however. Dozens more, from the Obituary Cocktail to the New Orleans Martini (this is made with Louisiana orange wine in place of vermouth), await the Bachelor in New Orleans at his pleasure.

For the guidance of the New Orleans Bachelor of recent vintage, a few of the more notable bars and bar-restaurants welcoming the Bachelor in New Orleans and specializing in the drinks that make the city New Orleans are listed as follows . . . . .

★ ★ ★ ★ ★

(Bars are not listed in order of importance, however, but according to location in the city.)

★ ★ ★ ★ ★

THE ROOSEVELT BAR

Just off the lobby in the Roosevelt Hotel, 122 Baronne Street, is perhaps the largest and fanciest drinkery in town. If by any chance the Bachelor in New Orleans should make headquarters of the hotel while visiting the city—that is, while baching—opportunity will knock frequently for a quick one, a long one, or several of both while entering, leaving or circling about. The Ramos Gin Fizz is the specialty of the house.

THE SAZERAC BAR

At 300 Carondelet Street, is man's domain and dear to the heart of every male Bachelor in New Orleans worthy of the name. Here is served the Sazerac Cocktail as it is made from the original and now secret recipe. Ladies are not welcome—save on Mardi Gras Day.

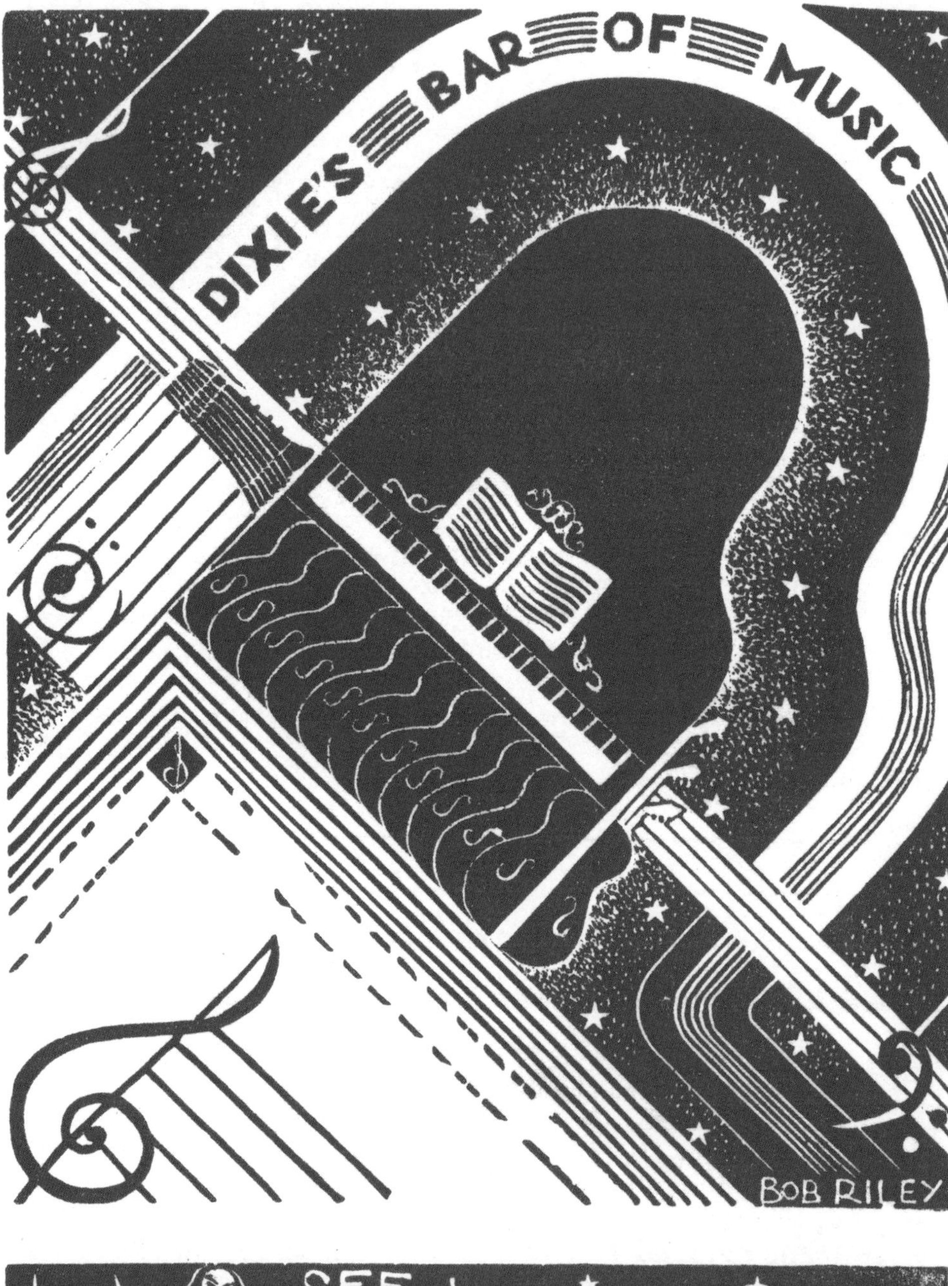
DIXIE'S BAR OF MUSIC
BOB RILEY

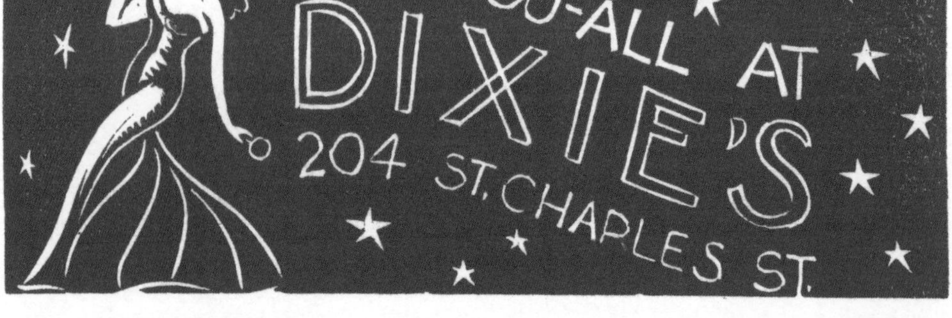
SEE YOU-ALL AT
DIXIE'S
204 ST. CHARLES ST.

★ ★ ★ ★ ★

Fellow Bachelors, meet your peer; JEAN LAFITTE!!

No wonder the "CASQUETTE BRIDES" left France; EVANGELINE shook GABRIEL; Bloody duels climaxed the "QUADROON BALLS" and MARIE LAVEAU chanted VOODOO!!!!

Meet the debonair LAFITTE surrounded by these gals at

The Doll House

Ma: 3500 640 Royal

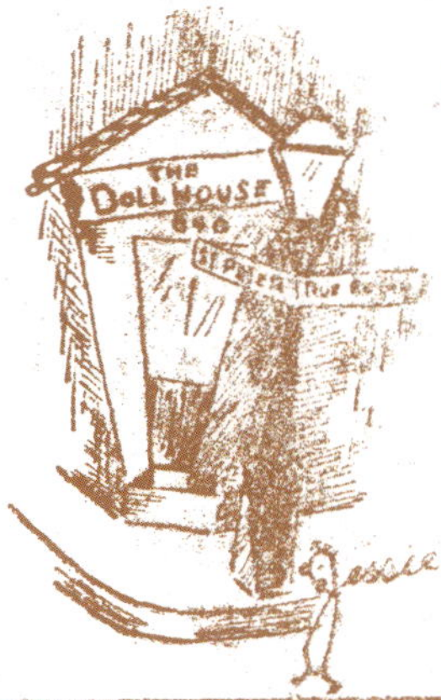

★ ★ ★ ★ ★

★ ★ ★ ★ ★

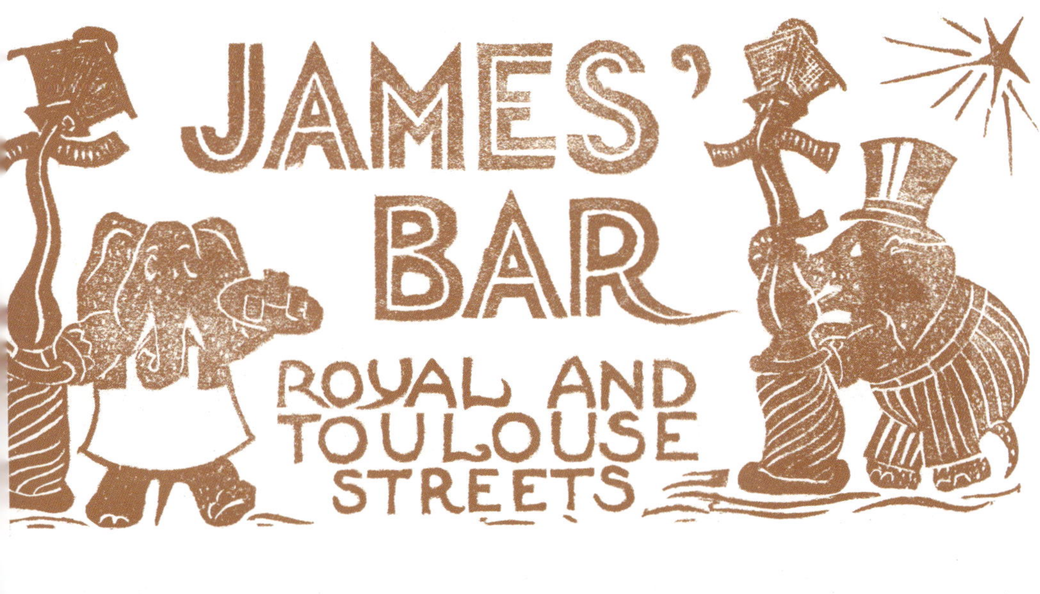

THE ST. CHARLES BAR

In the St. Charles Hotel, 211 St. Charles Street, has a history that, save for a polite gap during the lamentable Volstead days, stretches way back. There was a St. Charles Hotel in New Orleans famous by the time of the War Between the States *(never* call it the Civil War down here, not even in fun!), and its bar grew with it. Specialties here are the ingratiating Planter's Punch and the Old Fashioned Cocktail. There is music here for your entertainment during the Cocktail Hours, which are from 4:30 to 7:00 evenings.

DIXIE'S BAR OF MUSIC

204 St. Charles Street, is a tiny but cleverly decorated drinkery popular with Bachelors in New Orleans for its atmosphere of intimate gaiety. Clever Hollywood caricature murals by Xavier Gonzales back the bar, specialty of the house is the ultra potent "Soixante Neuf". Informal entertainment and music is offered for Bachelor pleasure. Dixie, herself, does a *mean* clarinet and vocalizes indigo.

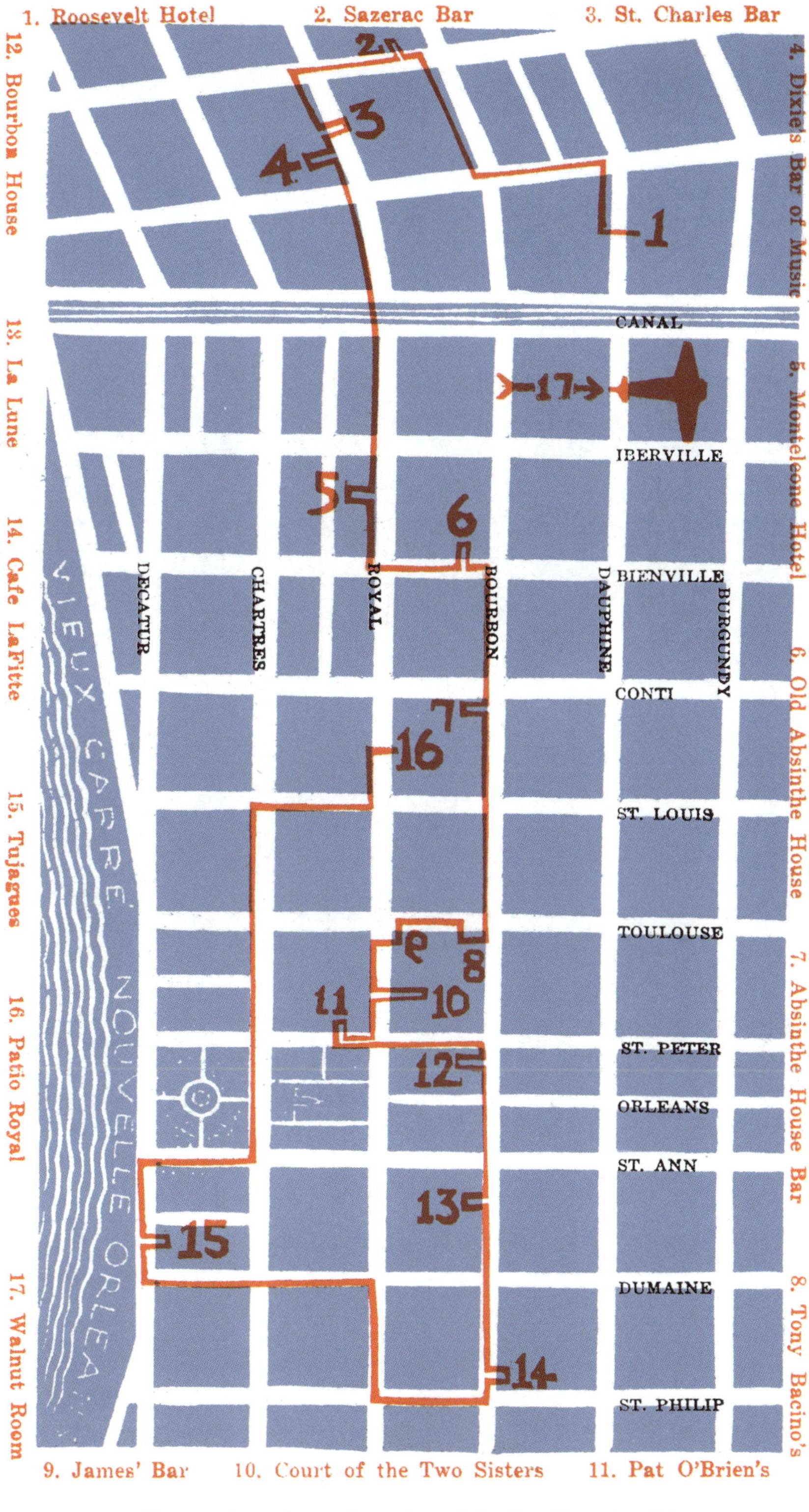

(If you don't know how to get to the Bars by this diagram . . . you'll have to start from somewhere else)

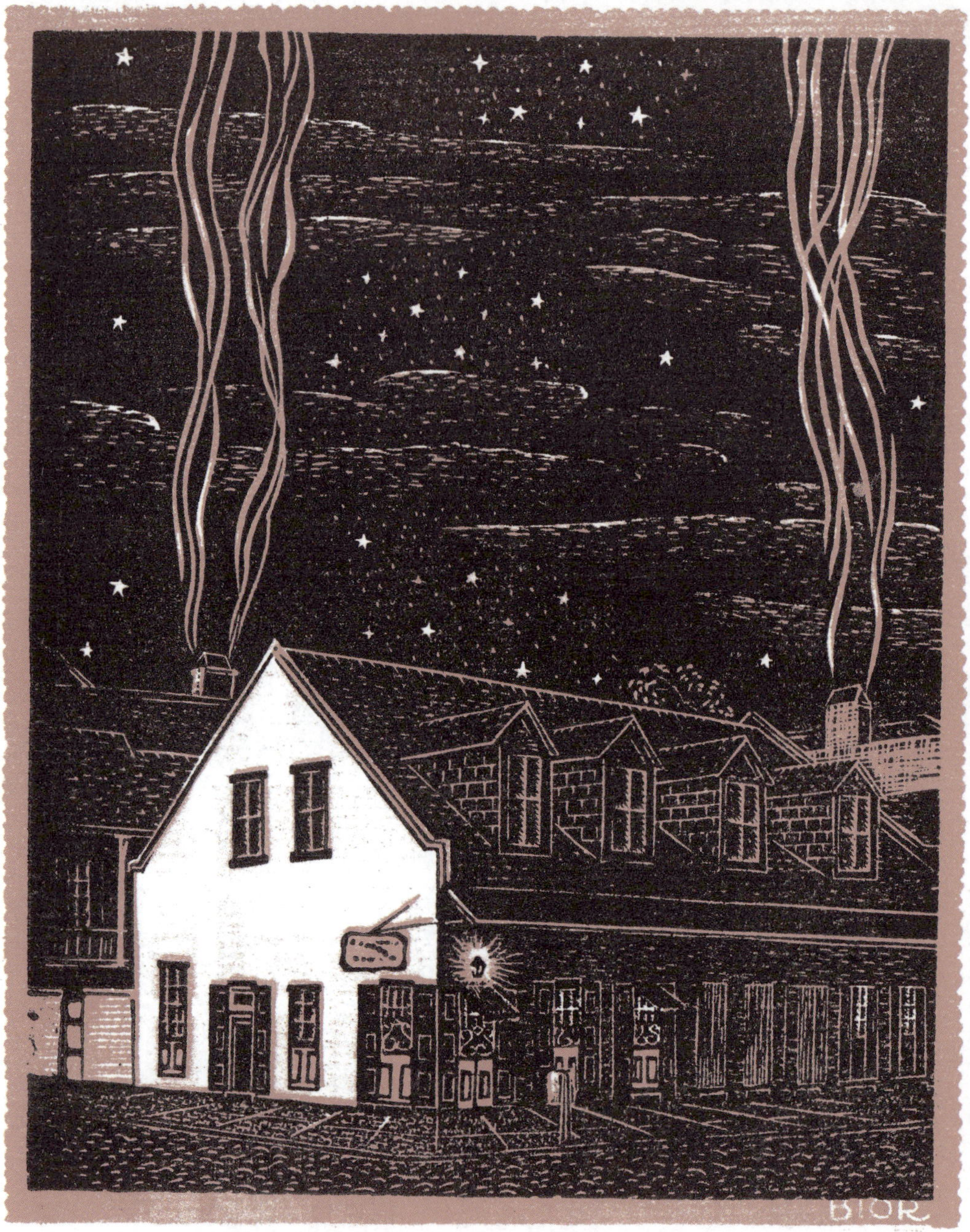

★ You can always have a good time at ★

TONY BACINO'S BAR
BOURBON AND TOULOUSE

Across the street from the site of the
OLD FRENCH OPERA HOUSE

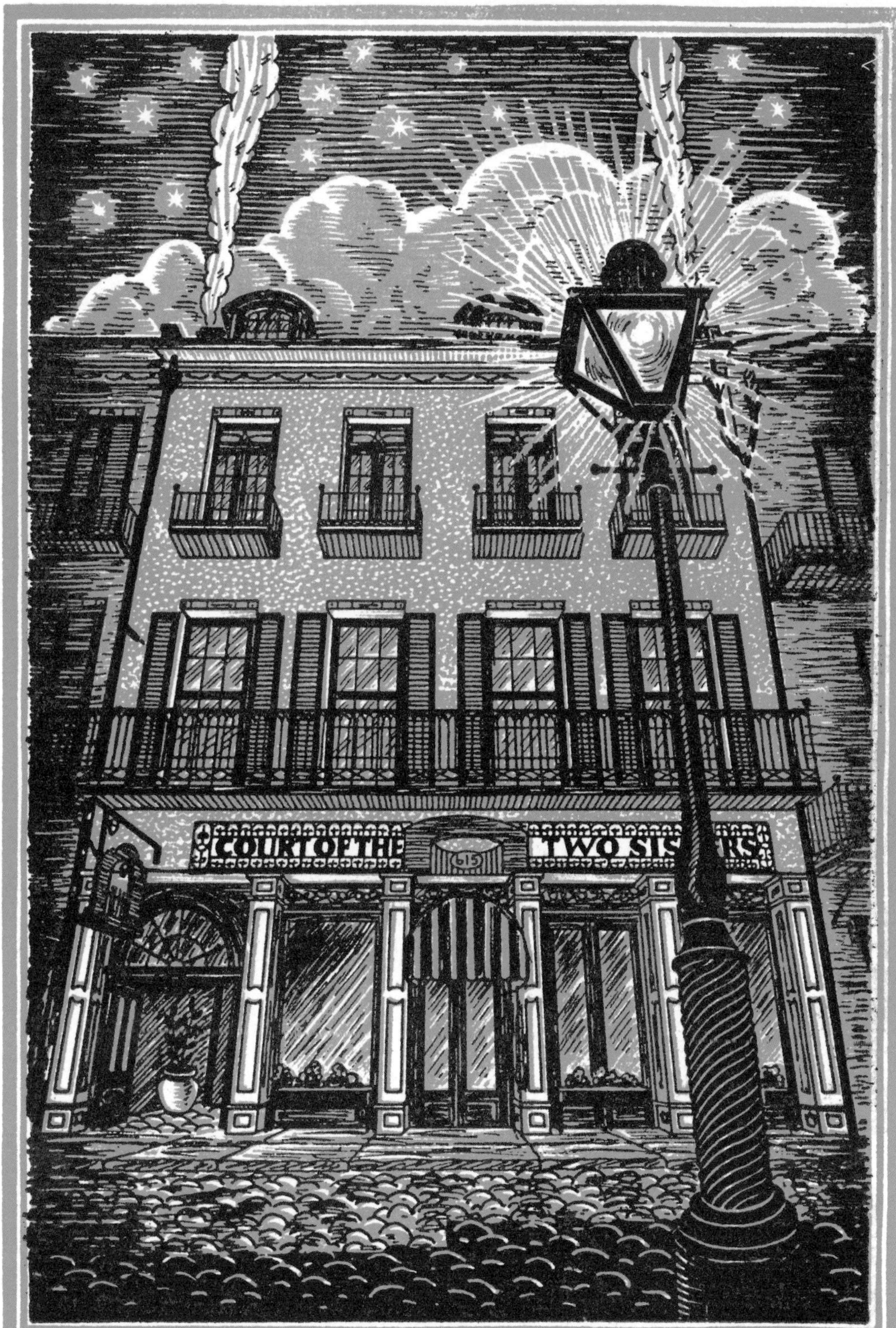

THE COURT OF THE TWO SISTERS

613 ROYAL STREET -:- JIMMIE COOPER, Owner

THE MONTELEONE HOTEL BAR

In the Monteleone Hotel, 214 Royal Street, also is large and of the metropolitan cocktail lounge type known as "smart". Here the Vieux Carre Cocktail is the specialty of the house. On the edge of the French Quarter, the Monteleone Hotel Bar is not a bad place to begin the plunge into Vieux Carre night-life. It is one of the last outposts of the re-assuring un-eccentric below Canal Street. Here you can take a deep breath before taking the fatal step.

THE OLD ABSINTHE HOUSE

238 Bourbon Street, has been a place of drink and fanciful doings of one sort and another practically since the day in 1798 when it was erected. Open from early in the morning until early in the morning, so to speak, night club entertainment is offered in the back rooms after dark.

THE ABSINTHE HOUSE BAR

400 Bourbon Street, not to be confused with the establishment above, boasts the orig-

inal marble-topped bar once a part of the building at 238 Bourbon. Over this bar for many decades has passed to Bachelors in New Orleans the famous Absinthe frappe, and that drink, appropriately, is now the specialty of the house.[2]

TONY BACINO'S BAR

At the corner of Bourbon and Toulouse Streets, has been serving the Bachelor in New Orleans but two years yet has grown rapidly so popular that Tony has been forced to add back rooms to take care of the overflow. "Hot piano" entertainment is offered in the club rooms at Tony Bacino's, as are various other diversions for the tippler who prefers to sit at the table.

JAMES' BAR

At the corner of Royal and Toulouse Streets, is one of the older established Quarter bars and notable for its air of quiet fun. Even on Saturday nights, James never sounds like hell on election day, and here many Bache-

(2) It is regrettable, perhaps, that the bar and the building have become separated.

lors in New Orleans hie themselves regularly to relax alcoholically in peace. A feature of this bar for music lovers is the large and well selected library of classical and semi-classical records, and at request any or several of eighty-seven fine albums will be played free of charge for your pleasure.

THE COURT OF THE TWO SISTERS

613 Royal Street, is notable for its bar as well as its excellent restaurant. An interesting and unusual decor suitable to its better-than-one-hundred years gives the court and building a rare charm. On warm nights, drinks are served in the candle-lit patio, and there is music for dancing.

PAT O'BRIEN'S BAR

At 638 St. Peter Street, just around the corner from Royal, is probably the most popular Saturday-night bar in the French Quarter. Many an exiled Bachelor in New Orleans at least once a week (Saturday nights, most often, of course!) weeps nostalgic tears for the old days at Pat's. Though Pat's is by no means a disreputable bar—quite the contrary is true—yet this bar is the happy place for Bachelors, men and women, of spirit and bravado. No soft lights and string music will be found here, friends. The spirit of Pat's is *robust!* Entertainment by a very remarkable girl-team at the piano, with songs and parodies, will make you remember Mercedes and Sue, of the back room, forever after a visit to Pat's.

THE BOURBON HOUSE BAR

At the corner of Bourbon and St. Peter Streets, is small and intimate, and here the less aggressive Bachelor in New Orleans will find his drinking hours very pleasant from the moment he enters, whereas in larger and more boisterous establishments it might take him some time to discover the distinction between New Orleans hospitality and total war. A place for quiet, leisurely sipping, The Bourbon House Bar, adjoining the Bourbon House Restaurant, has become practically the club of many Bachelors in New Orleans. (Some even get their mail here!)

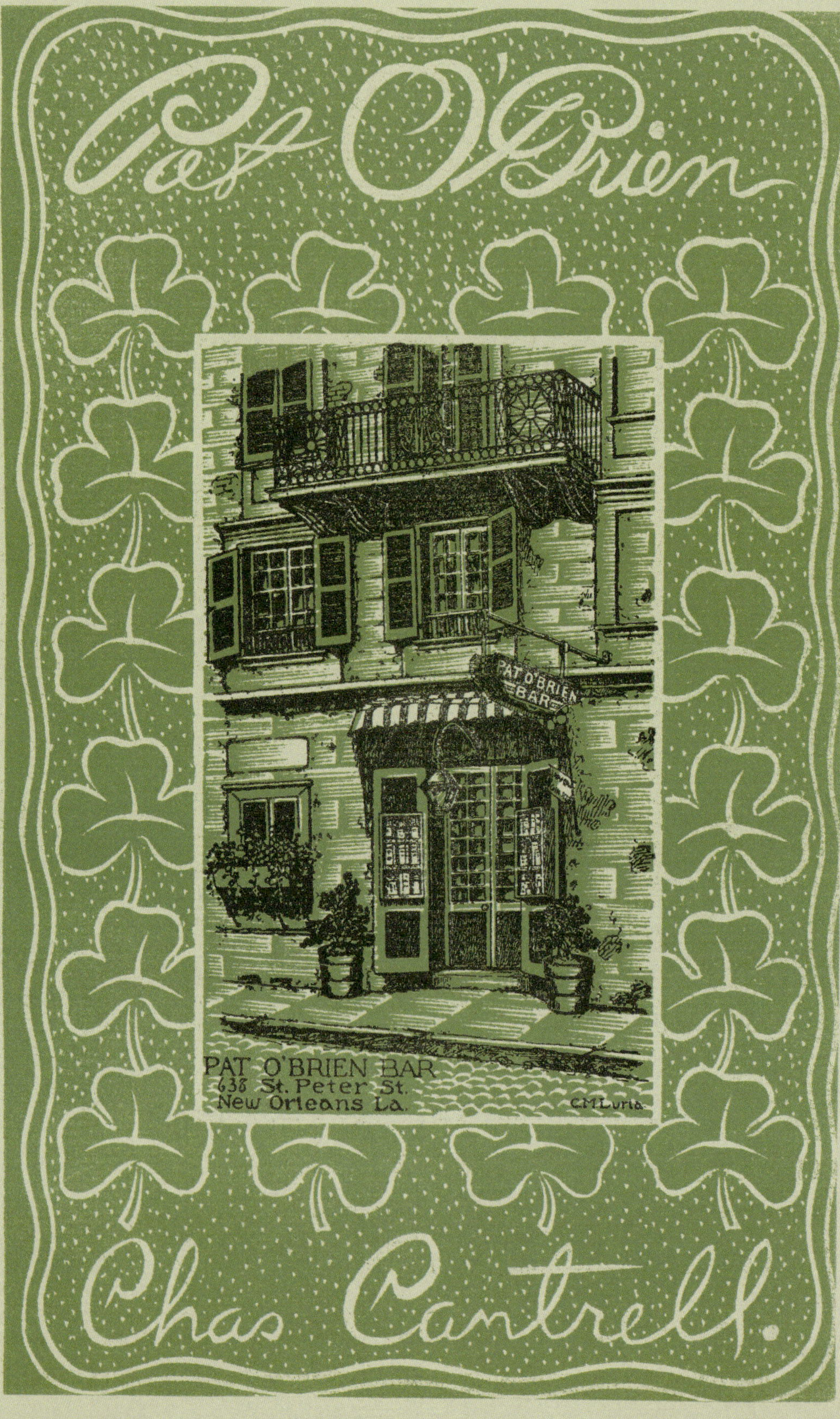
Pat O'Brien
PAT O'BRIEN BAR
PAT O'BRIEN BAR
638 St. Peter St.
New Orleans La.
C.M.Luria
Chas Cantrell.

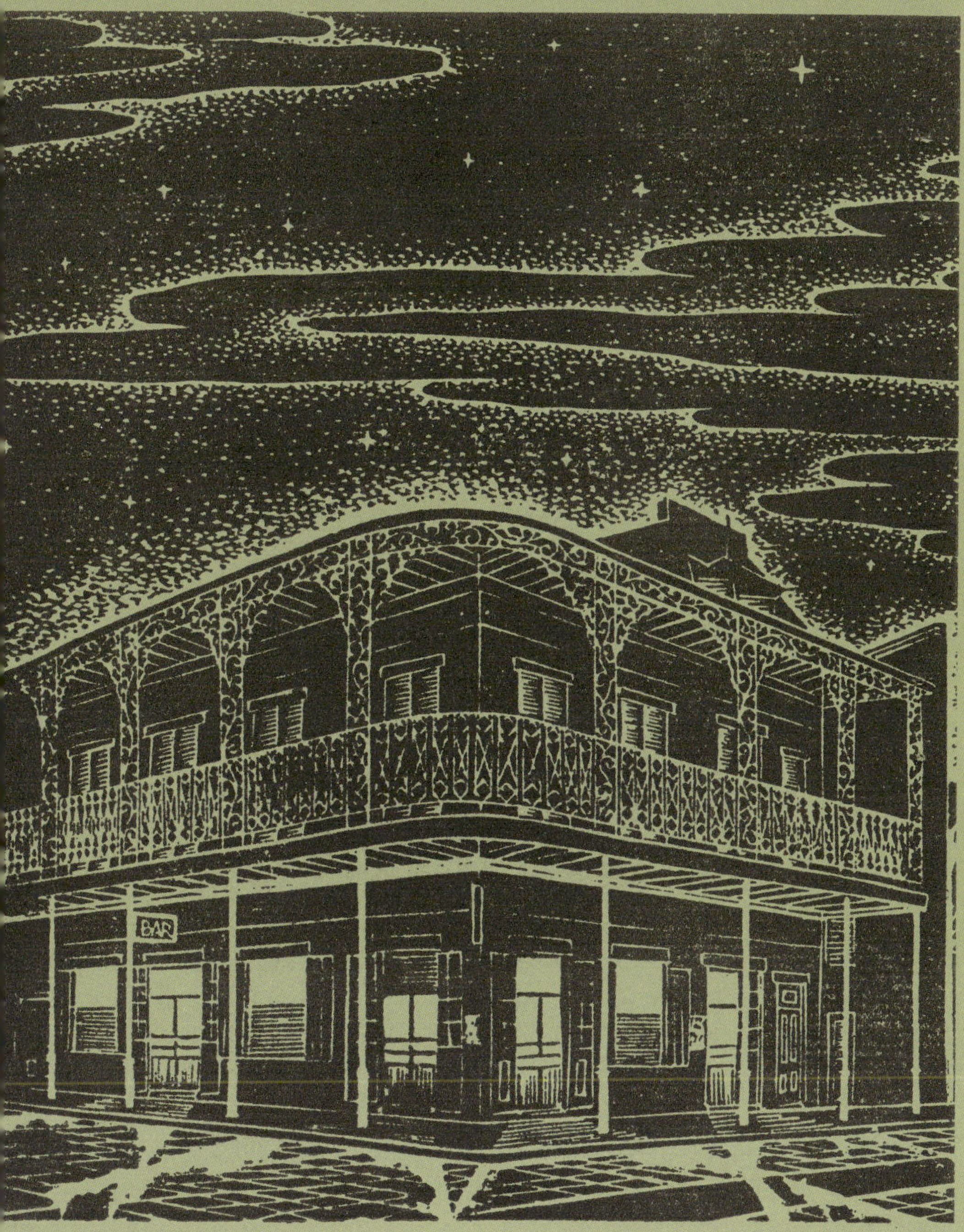

BOURBON HOUSE Inc

BOURBON AND ST. PETER

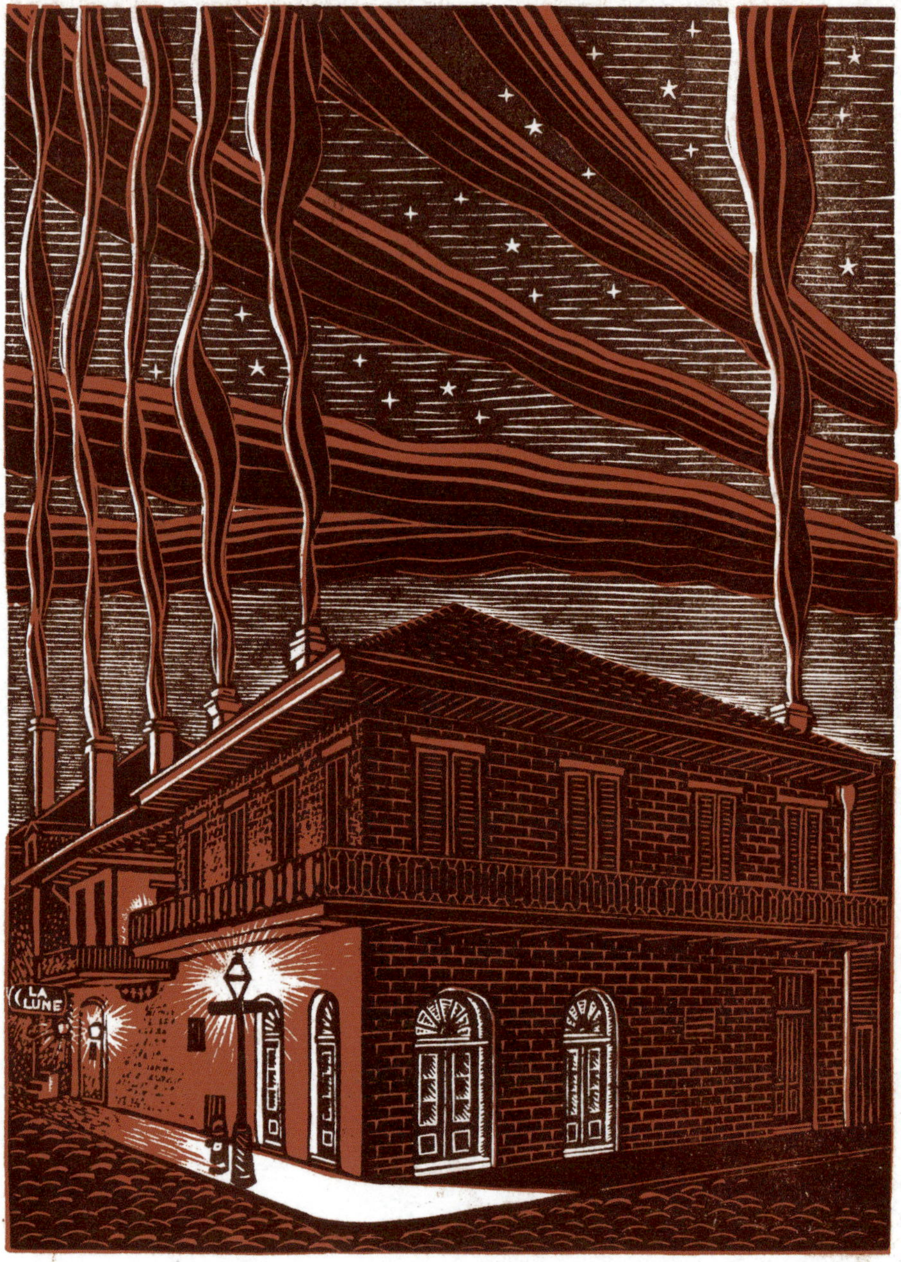

La Lune - Bourbon and St. Ann - New Orleans

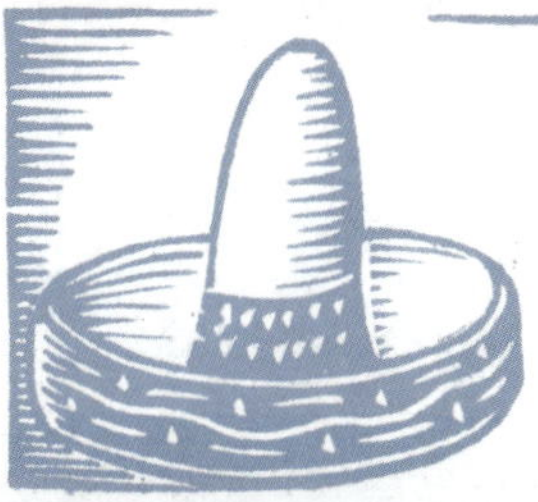

Where You Can

DRINK-DINE AND DANCE

In The Unusual Atmosphere Of

OLD MEXICO

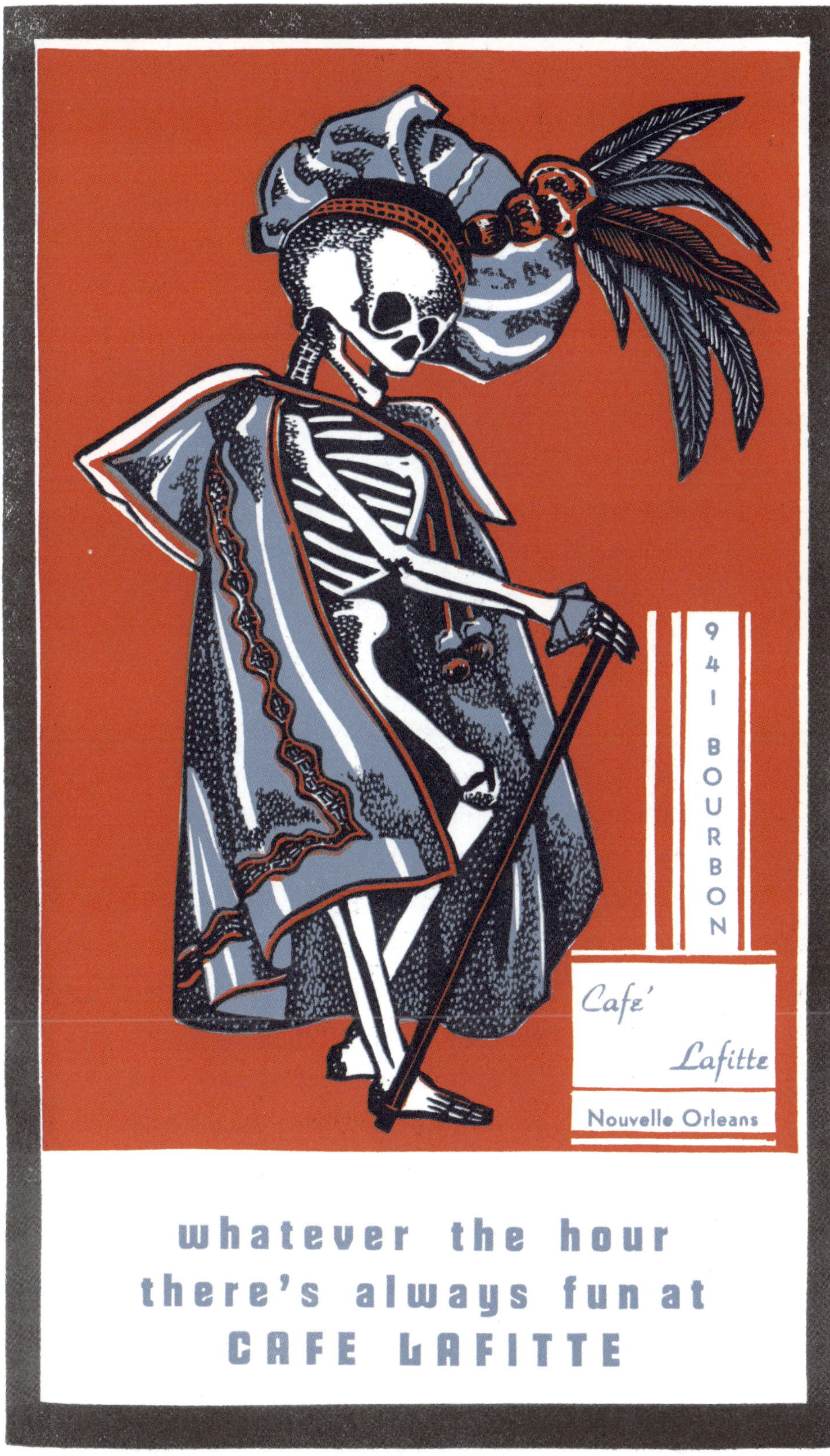
941 BOURBON
Café Lafitte
Nouvelle Orleans
whatever the hour
there's always fun at
CAFE LAFITTE

LA LUNE

At 800 Bourbon Street, is a bar and night club popular with those of the later evening crowd who prefer a touch of Latin (Mexican, in this case) with their elbow lifting. Pleasantly decorated throughout by Bob Riley, and displaying a very fine mural by Enrique Alferez, La Lune is practically a *must* on the nocturnal itinerary of any Bachelor in New Orleans. Music for the ears or feet is offered by a Mexican band. House specialty is the deceptive Tequila Sunrise.

CAFE LAFITTE

941 Bourbon Street, is one of the most unusual and charming restaurant-bars in New Orleans. The one-story brick building—now restored—was once occupied by pirate Jean Lafitte's blacksmith shop, which served as a respectable front, it is believed, for the pirate's thriving business in both yellow gold and black, the booty from plundered ships. The building is at least 169 years old. The specialties of Cafe Lafitte's excellently equipped bar are the dangerous Obituary

Cocktail and the Lafitte Special. An atmosphere of complete informality prevails here: if the bartender is passed out, go behind and mix your own! The bar is open twenty-four hours a day, and there are no keys to Cafe Lafitte's doors—it is rumored that Jean Lafitte tossed them away after three Obituaries!

TUJAGUE'S BAR

823 Decatur Street, opposite the French Market, is an old timey drinkery that pays little attention to fashions in bars. Here you will find no red leather bar stools, no super-duper fixtures. Here is drink served in the way and in the surroundings your father drank it. Specialty of the house is the Absinthe frappe.

THE WALNUT ROOM

Just off the main lobby of the New Orleans Airport, is dedicated to the Bachelor coming and going, but this pleasant, informal bar and club brings many Bachelors in New Orleans out from town for an afternoon or evening of ticketless sipping and dancing.

THE WALNUT ROOM

THE **DIFFERENT** BAR

AND NIGHT CLUB

AT THE CROSSROADS OF THE SKY!

Wing out to the New Orleans Airport, taxi across to the Walnut Room, and cut your gun, Bachelors! The Walnut Room offers superlative liquors and top dance music in an atmosphere of friendly gaiety. Open day and night for your pleasure and our own, the Walnut Room, at the New Orleans Airport, must be a **must** on your entertainment list.

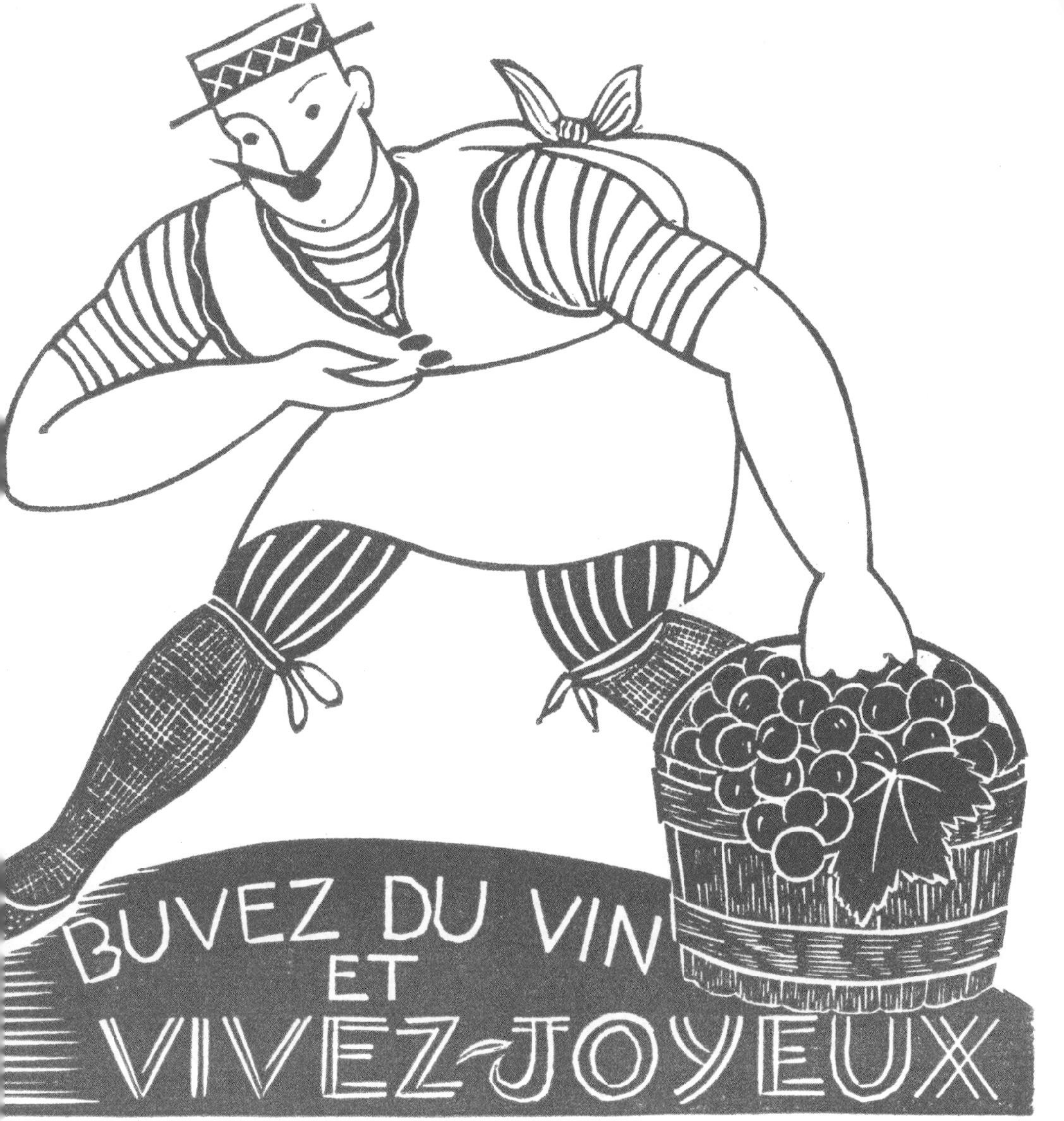

LE PETITE CAFE BAR
425 Rue Royale

Vieux Carre **New Orleans**

In Conjunction With

PATIO ROYAL

No doubt you know that the Patio Royal is one of the distinctive restaurants in the old French Quarter and boasts of the excellency as to French and Creole cuisine.

Gentlemen Bachelors will like the costumes—or lack of them! - - - of the pretty Stewardettes; ladies will find the decor attractive and will feel pleasantly at home in the atmosphere of simple friendliness. Announcing their specialty as the Volga Boatman, a Vodka-base thriller, the management remarks that customers are not served less than a pair!

Music of considerable heat is offered for dancing, and with this music mingles the singing of one of the handsomest blonde dollies that ever a Bachelor set eyes upon.

LE PETITE CAFE BAR

In the PATIO ROYAL, in the 400 block of Royal Street, is a small but extremely well appointed bar. One of the smarter Quarter spots, this bar-lounge makes a particularly appropriate rendezvous for intimate conversations. The tasteful decorations were done by Bob Riley.

(This is one time when the *last* is the *least* Bar mentioned)

★ ★ ★ ★ ★

★ ★ ★ ★ ★

Bachelors must remember, however, that the bars listed above are but a few of the thousands awaiting them in New Orleans. Also, though the bars above are particularly distinguished, in one way or another, as drinkeries, there are others in numbers that merit attention we have not space for here.

Before we close this chapter, Bachelors in New Orleans, let us pour a glass between us and toast one fine friend we all have, and one who is practically unsung: your bartender and mine!

Long may he pour our drinks!

★ ★ ★ ★ ★

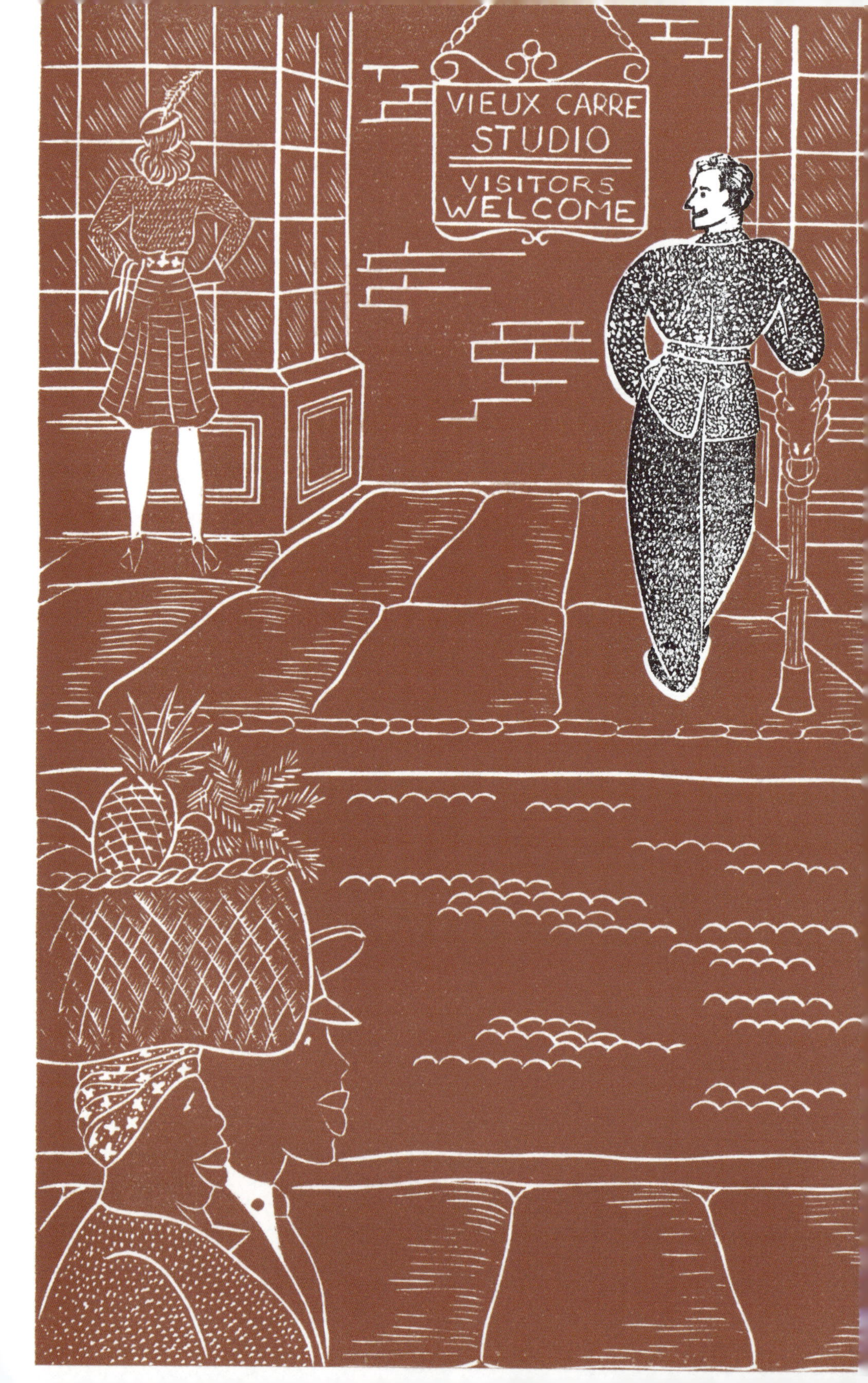
VIEUX CARRE
STUDIO
VISITORS
WELCOME

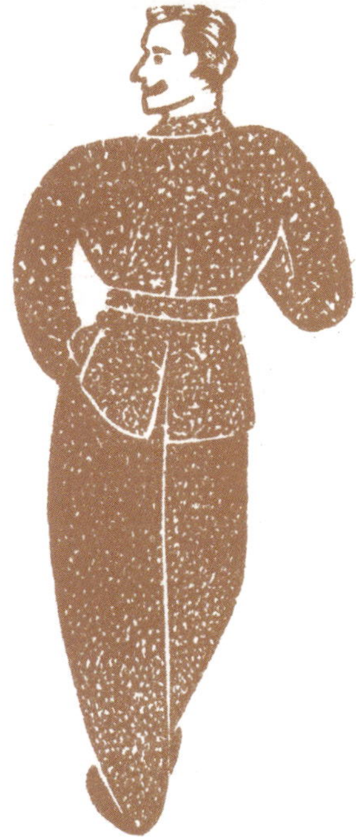

DONT BE A TOURIST

CHAPTER TWO

Somehow, the word *tourist* carries, in New Orleans, at least, most unpleasant implications. A tourist is a peeker into private doings, a gawker at buildings, a person who appears thoroughly eager to be scandalized. A tourist is, in short, a nub. He is gummy, a bane to civilization. He elbows peaceful souls off the sidewalk when he is sober, and when he is intoxicated he kicks garbage cans and insults street-walkers.

The Bachelor in New Orleans is not a tourist. The tourist is never a Bachelor in New Orleans. The Bachelor in New Orleans may he a visitor; he or she may admire the city's beautiful architecture; and yet the Bachelor never for a moment is a tourist. Make no mistake about this.

Yet until the Bachelor in New Orleans becomes known about the town, he has, so to speak, to prove himself. There are certain things that might be done that would confuse others, that might make them mistake him for a tourist. To be mistaken for a tourist is most embarrassing.

To avoid this horror, you should keep a few rules in mind. The following list of *don'ts* will help:

1. Never, never kick garbage cans! This is a cardinal sin for Bachelors in New Orleans.

2. Speak kindly to prostitutes, should you encounter them, unless they paw you. They work hard, poor creatures, and probably approve just as little of their trade as do you.

After all, why shouldn't they: they know more about it. However, let's not cry in our beers.

3. Above all, be nice to your bartender, unless he slips you a Mickey Finn. If you aren't nice to him, he might anyway—or at least, it would be a good idea.

4. Never stand and stare at any happening, no matter how rare, outrageous, unseemly, or unconventional it may strike you. If an unusual happening is pleasant or gay, a New Orleans Bachelor unobtrusively takes part in it; if it is unpleasant, the Bachelor in New Orleans unobtrusively takes part in something else.

5. Never buy someone a drink without first asking him if he wants it. He is bound to feel that he must buy you one back, and if he should happen not to have any money on him, he will not love you. The true Bachelor in New Orleans desires very much to be loved.

6. Do not consider that since you are in the "deep South" you have a right to play

Simon Legree to Negroes at any time or in any place. You will find that Southern ladies and gentlemen, if they are not what black and white alike call "white trash," treat Negroes with great courtesy and consideration. If you should go to a Negro night club, by the way, it is highly important, to your skin as to your manners, to behave yourself.

7. Never raise your voice above Martha Ray's level. People across the river and in adjoining parishes have to sleep. In the French Quarter, of course, no one could sleep if a sudden quiet fell in the streets. Bed-occupiers would sit bolt upright, in a cold sweat!

8. Never ask an interesting looking individual if he is an artist. He might be one, in which case he will resent you. And if he is not, he may cause you some embarrassment.

9. Do not attempt to direct traffic or dance bands while over-intoxicated. You will not do your best job if you have had one too many, and a most remarkable and unpleasant snarl may result.

10. If you are a male Bachelor, never make what could be considered the first pass at any woman you have not known all your life. If she is interested, or *can* be satisfactorily interested, she will make the first pass—and if you are a Bachelor in New Orleans, you will know when it happens. Also, if she has a husband—and you *never* know!—he will be more liable (that is, you have a chance) to beat her before he gets to you, and meanwhile you can be finding a taxi. This rule does not apply to female Bachelors in New Orleans: being females, they have their own rules about these matters and do what they're going to do anyway.

At any rate, don't be a tourist.

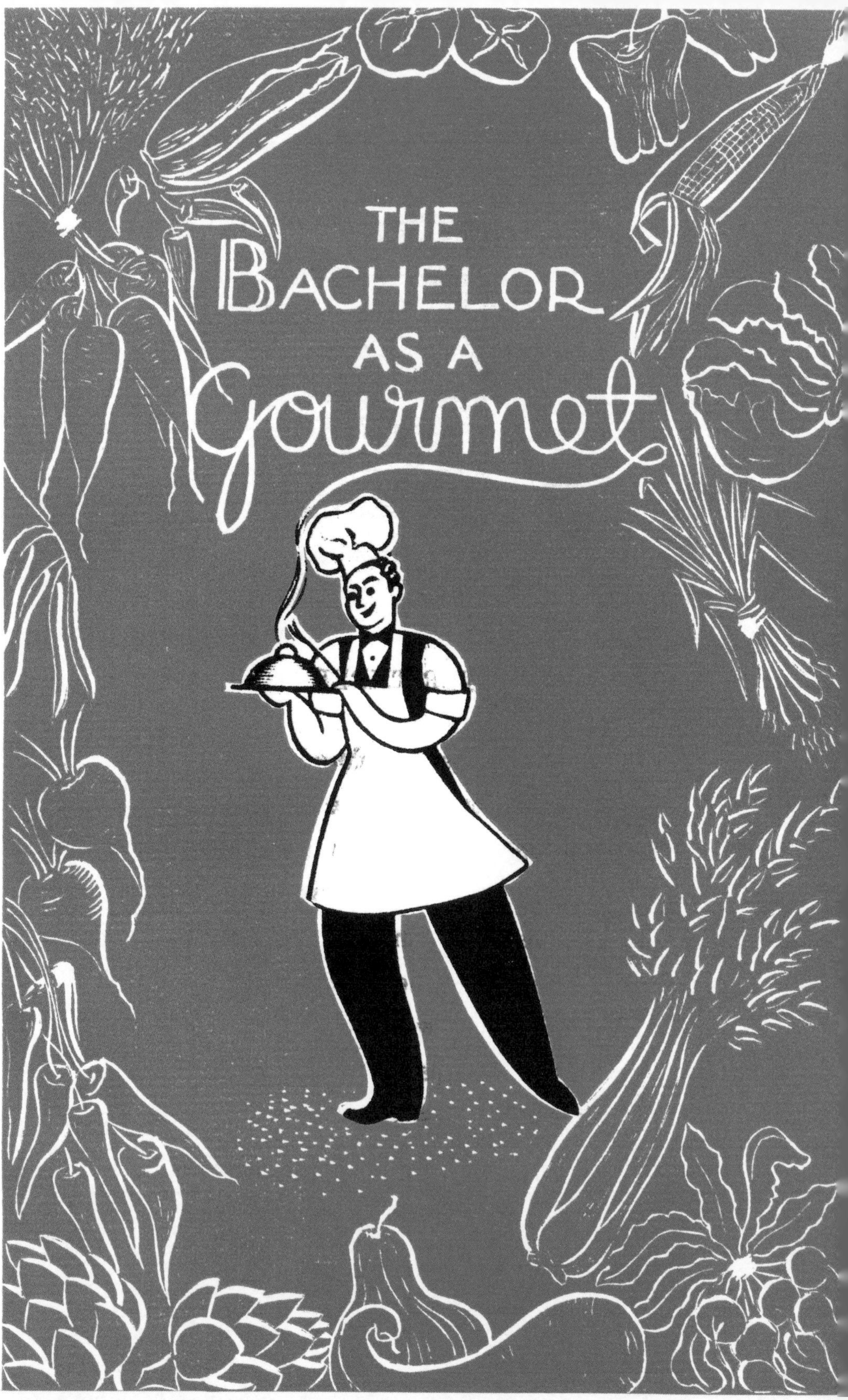
THE
BACHELOR
AS A
Gourmet

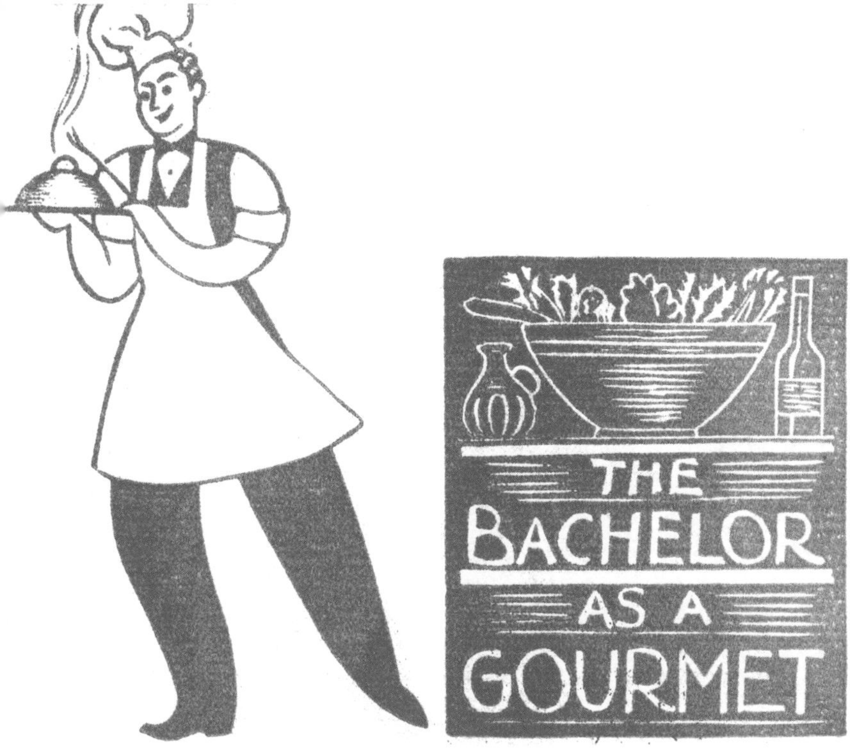

CHAPTER THREE

Numberless are the Bachelors in New Orleans of former years, many of them internationally famous men, who have grown speechless with rapture at the very mention of New Orleans restaurants and the food they serve. That great Bachelor in New Orleans of yesteryear, Mark Twain, went so far as to call baked Gulf pompano, "delicious as the less criminal forms of sin," and that, as every Bachelor in New Orleans knows, is good!

The city has been famous for its unique dishes for more than a century. To New Orleans, the early French brought their native culinary arts, and here they found new herbs, new spices, new seafood and new vegetables with which to create highly original cookery. When the Spanish came, they added here and there touches of Latin heat to the dishes; and later, when Negro kitchen genius became recognized, African subtleties were blended with the rest to form the whole of our famous New Orleans food.

It was not until the greatly prosperous eighteen-thirties that New Orleans restaurants came into their own, however, for before this time most dining was at private homes.

By 1856, when the great author William Makepeace Thackery visited New Orleans and recorded his delight in the city, the distinction of the restaurants was pronounced. "At that comfortable tavern on Pontchartrain," Thackery said, "we had a bouillabaisse than which a better was never eaten at Marseille —and not the least headache in the morning," he added happily.

Antoine's, New Orleans' most famous restaurant even today, was established in the present building by the late great chef Antoine Alciatore in 1876, and its cuisine is representative of the best served in the great New Orleans restaurants in the century of their fame.

Irvin S. Cobb, that genial Bachelor in New Orleans and great American humorist, wrote: ". . . I made a special trip to a certain cafe in Paris to eat bouillabaisse. I found it distinctly worthwhile. Later, I went to Marseilles, the home of this dish, and found it better. And then I came back to America and ate it in Antoine's in New Orleans and found it best of all."

Will Rogers, too, raved about the victuals. "Why, listen," he crowed, "they got a soup they herded around in front of me that was crawfish boiled in white wine and aromatic herbs. Why, they got tortoiseshell terrapin served in its own shell. Omelette soufflee historiee! Say, they make all of them out of golden pheasants' eggs."

New Orleans cuisine specialties include the famous *huitres en coquille a la Rockefeller*, Oysters Rockefeller to you; *pompano en papillote*, a delectable Gulf fish cooked in a sealed paper bag with an incomparable sauce; *bouillabaisse*, the multi-fish soup or stew that so enchanted Mr. Thackery and Mr. Cobb; *court-bouillon*, a redfish dish; *crayfish bisque*, another famous soup; *gumbo*, a wonderful concoction made with crabs, shrimp and oysters; and of course, *red beans and rice*, which is what it implies but surprisingly palatable.

The fine restaurants in New Orleans today are as numerous as the excellent bars and should be visited with perhaps more reverence. We have mentioned Antoine's as one of the oldest and as perhaps the most famous today, but smaller restaurants and the hotel dining rooms offer frequently superb cuisine and often at more convenient prices.

The restaurants mentioned in the following list are outstanding of their kind, but there are others we have not sufficient space to list here, and many of them serve excellent food.

ANTOINE'S

713 St. Louis Street, near the uptown edge of the French Quarter, offers a vast menu, entirely *a la carte,* of superlative French and Creole dishes. The restaurant is rather expensive, but many Bachelors in New Orleans go to Antoine's as pilgrims to a shrine, and consider the cost as nothing. There is a minimum charge of $1.00 per person. Dinner here is an experience the Bachelor in New Orleans will never, never forget.

ARNAUD'S

813 Bienville Street, is young to have become such a distinguished New Orleans restaurant (established 1921), but in the short space of two decades has grown quite famous for its French and Creole cuisine. Specialties here include the delicious shrimps Arnaud, *crepe suzette* Arnaud, breast of turkey *en papillote, filet de truite* Amandine, oyster Whitney, stuffed crab Rejane, and *langouste* Sarah Bernhardt.

BROUSSARD'S

819 Conti Street, is a small and unpretentious restaurant but noted for its delicately prepared food and excellent service. In pleasant weather, dinner is served in a charming garden courtyard. Specialties are the Broussard Surprise, a desert; chicken *papillote;* and oysters *a la* Broussard. Private dining rooms are available for parties, but reservations should be made.

CAFE LAFITTE

941 Bourbon, we have mentioned in some detail in Chapter One, but the restaurant is by no means less distinguished than the bar. At pleasant informal tables, diners have a choice of many well-cooked and beautifully served Creole and French dishes. Cafe Lafitte's Special Steak Dinner, too, is particularly recommendable. This is one of the comparatively few restaurants in New Orleans where a really worth while steak can be ordered, by the way.

THE COURT OF THE TWO SISTERS

615 Royal Street, offers excellent French and Creole cooking in a dining atmosphere of great charm. In pleasant weather, dinner is served in the courtyard at candle-lighted tables, as well as in the patio and in the handsome dining room at the front. There are numerous seafood and chicken specialties of distinction. There is generally an orchestra for dancing.

GALATOIRE'S

209 Bourbon Street, is another comparatively unpretentious French restaurant popular with gourmets. Particularly delicious here is the Dinkelspiel salad, a huge affair made of crabmeat and garrisonned by *hors d'oeuvres.*

In New Orleans, a French restaurant is not considered a foreign one. However, Italian, Mexican, German, and Chinese restaurants are to be found in numbers in New Orleans. A few of the more distinguished follow.

The Court of the Two Sisters. The name was gained from the fact that two sisters, members of an aristocratic family of Old New Orleans, here conducted a fancy and variety store for a period of years. The present structure, three stories and attic, was erected in 1832 by Zenon Cavalier, financier of note in the early days of Louisiana history, and a Colonel in the American forces in the War of 1812. Prior to this, the site was occupied as the residence of Sieur Etienne De Perier, Governor of the French Colonial period—1725-1733, succeeding Bienville, Governor General, founder of New Orleans (1718). De Perier was a tireless and energetic administrator and was noted for distributing rewards and punishment with equal impartiality. Of particular interest and charm is the picturesque courtyard, the most spacious patio in the historic center of the Old French Quarter. During the earlier days this courtyard was a pleasant retreat for family privacy and also served as a delightful cooling system that was ideally adapted to a warm, moist climate.

- **Restful relaxation**
- **Favorite drinks**
- **Authentic cuisine**
- **Dancing . . . in mellow candle light . . beneath the willows and stars**
- **Romantic music . . . . by Johnny Miller and his orchestra**

- **THE COURT OF THE TWO SISTERS**
  613 Royal St.
- **JIMMIE COOPER, your host . . . .**

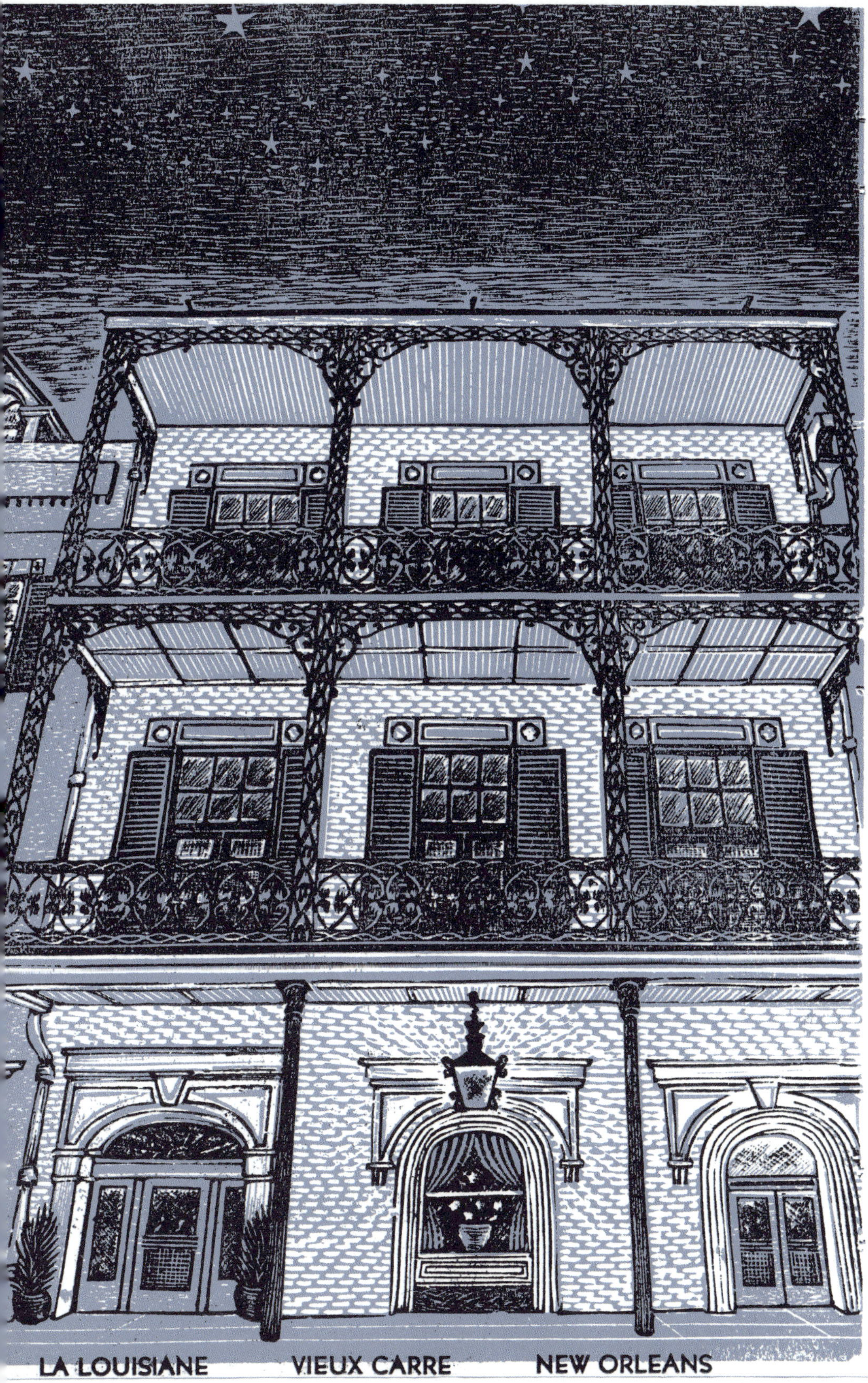

LA LOUISIANE VIEUX CARRE NEW ORLEANS

KOLB'S

125 St. Charles Street, is a German-American restaurant of great distinction. Here are served such specialties as stewed goose with dumplings; pig knuckles with sauerkraut; and wiener schnitzel. An orchestra provides entertainment for evening guests, who are invited to join in the singing of folk songs.

LA LOUISIANE

725 Iberville Street, was established in 1881 and since has maintained its distinction as a fine and luxurious restaurant. More than most of the better New Orleans restaurants, La Louisiane tends to elegance in its furnishings and general decor. The building which it occupies, too, is noteworthy for its beauty. Specialties of La Louisiane include *filet de truite marguery; bisque ecrevisse Louisiane;* turkey Rochambeau; and *canape* crab Louisiane.

LA LUNE

800 Bourbon Street, is popular for its excellent Mexican dishes as well as for its bar. The chicken tacos are particularly good. A

spirited Mexican dance band plays nightly, and the dance floor is excellent.

MADAME BEGUE'S

504 Madison Street, across from the French Market, has been famous for its six-course breakfasts—with endlessly flowing wine—since well before 1900. These breakfasts early were sumptuous affairs, lasting from midmorning until well into the afternoon. The specialty of Madame Begue's in its heyday (when it was known simply as Begue's) was the breakfast of which kidney stew with red wine was the main course. The poet Eugene Field, an early Bachelor in New Orleans, frequented this restaurant in the Nineties when he was a visitor to the city. Breakfast prices start at one dollar, but these breakfasts mean *food!*

MASERA'S

807 St. Louis Street, is one of the more popular of the many New Orleans restaurants distinguished for its Italian specialties.

MONTALBANO'S

724 St. Philip Street, is a highly unusual combination of restaurant, delicatessen, and shrine. The dining room, known as the Roma Room, was blessed by Pope Pius XI and contains a small but elaborate altar at the top of which is a replica of the Vatican. As very few guests can be seated at one time, it is best to make reservations for a party.

THE MORNING CALL COFFEE STAND AND RESTAURANT

Situated in the front of the first building on the uptown side of the French Market, is one of several New Orleans restaurants in a class by themselves. From the earliest days of the French Market, farmers and fishermen bringing vegetables, meats, and seafood to the Market before dawn frequented little coffee stalls and restaurants in this sector, and these establishments have become noted for their good, solid cooking and their excellent French coffee, which they still offer at surprisingly low prices. The Morning Call has grown popular in recent years with the "uptown crowd," which mingles with the cajun farmer and fisherfolk in the wee sma' hours.

THE PATIO ROYAL RESTAURANT

In the 400 block of Royal Street across from the Court House, is situated in one of the handsomest and most charming buildings in the French Quarter. The building was once the home of Paul Morphy, an international chess champion whose wizardry with queens, knights and pawns brought him lasting fame. French and Creole dishes, served with old world graciousness, are the specialty of the restaurant.

THE PONTALBA TEA ROOM

On the corner of St. Peter and Chartres Streets at Jackson Square, is a quiet and dignified dining room popular with patrician New Orleanians. Miss Lottie Mitchell, the charming proprietress, makes a specialty of catering to weddings and formal parties, so if the Bachelor wishes to entertain privately, he would do well to consult her.

TUJAGUE'S

823 Decatur Street, across the street from the French Market, has been in business since 1880 and still has some of the flavor of the smaller restaurants of the Nineties. The cooking is distinctly French—but unadorned and solid. The comfortable and unpretentious dining room compliments nicely the old-fashioned bar adjoining. Both restaurant and bar close rather early—about nine-thirty, generally—so keep this in mind when you make your plans for dinner.

THE ROOSEVELT HOTEL

Offers several distinguished restaurants for the pleasure of hungry but discriminating Bachelors in New Orleans. The Roosevelt is noted for the care and expense devoted to the maintaining of its superb staff of chefs. Here the chef is "topman," no fooling! The Roosevelt specializes in the outstanding dishes of old France and Creole Louisiana and is a favorite haunt of gourmets.

TURCI'S ITALIAN GARDENS

223 Bourbon Street, established by Signor

and Signora Turci some years ago when they retired from distinguished careers in opera, is a favorite restaurant of singers and musicians. Specialties are ravioli and spaghetti.

★ ★ ★ ★ ★

Before closing this chapter on New Orleans restaurants and food, let us add one pleading word.

Bachelors, food, in New Orleans, is not something you eat to keep from being hungry. Eating here, though not necessarily a solemn business, is something of a sacred ritual.

Don't get in a hurry when you are in the neighborhood of a fine restaurant. If you *have* to rush, pick up a sandwich at some drugstore—and eat, that is, *really* eat later when you have time to be courteous to your food.

Don't get *too* drunk just before ordering an excellent dinner. It just isn't fair to the chef. He'll want to cry, or to chop at you with a cleaver. Both results are embarrassing.

Don't raise hell at the table. Raise hell at the bar, if you like, but to shout at or over oysters Rockefeller is to identify yourself as a boor or a hag-souled, fishwifely bitch.

In short, be kind to your food, and it will love you. So will the chef.

★ ★ ★ ★ ★

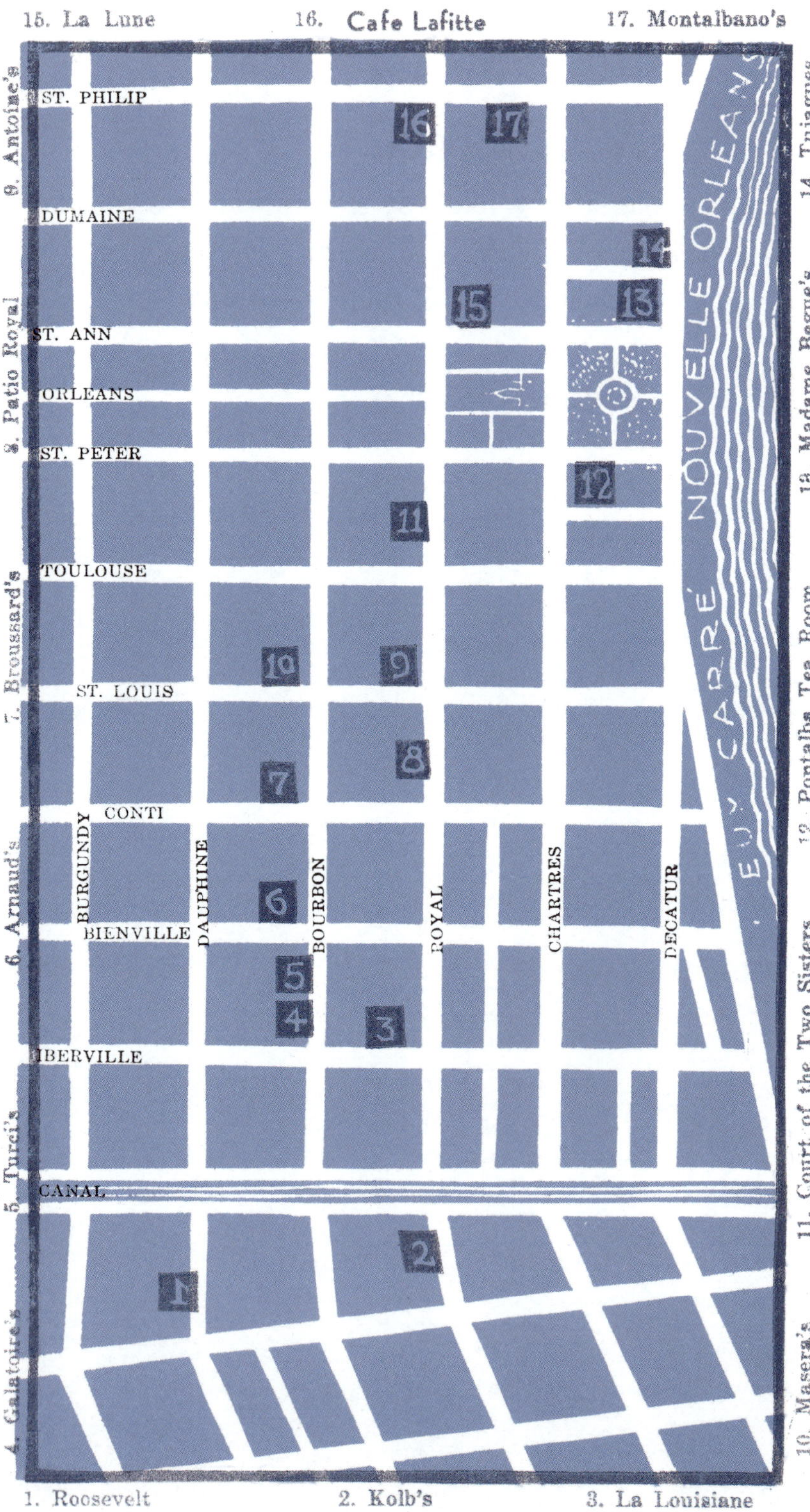

This diagram shows location of restaurants mentioned herein.

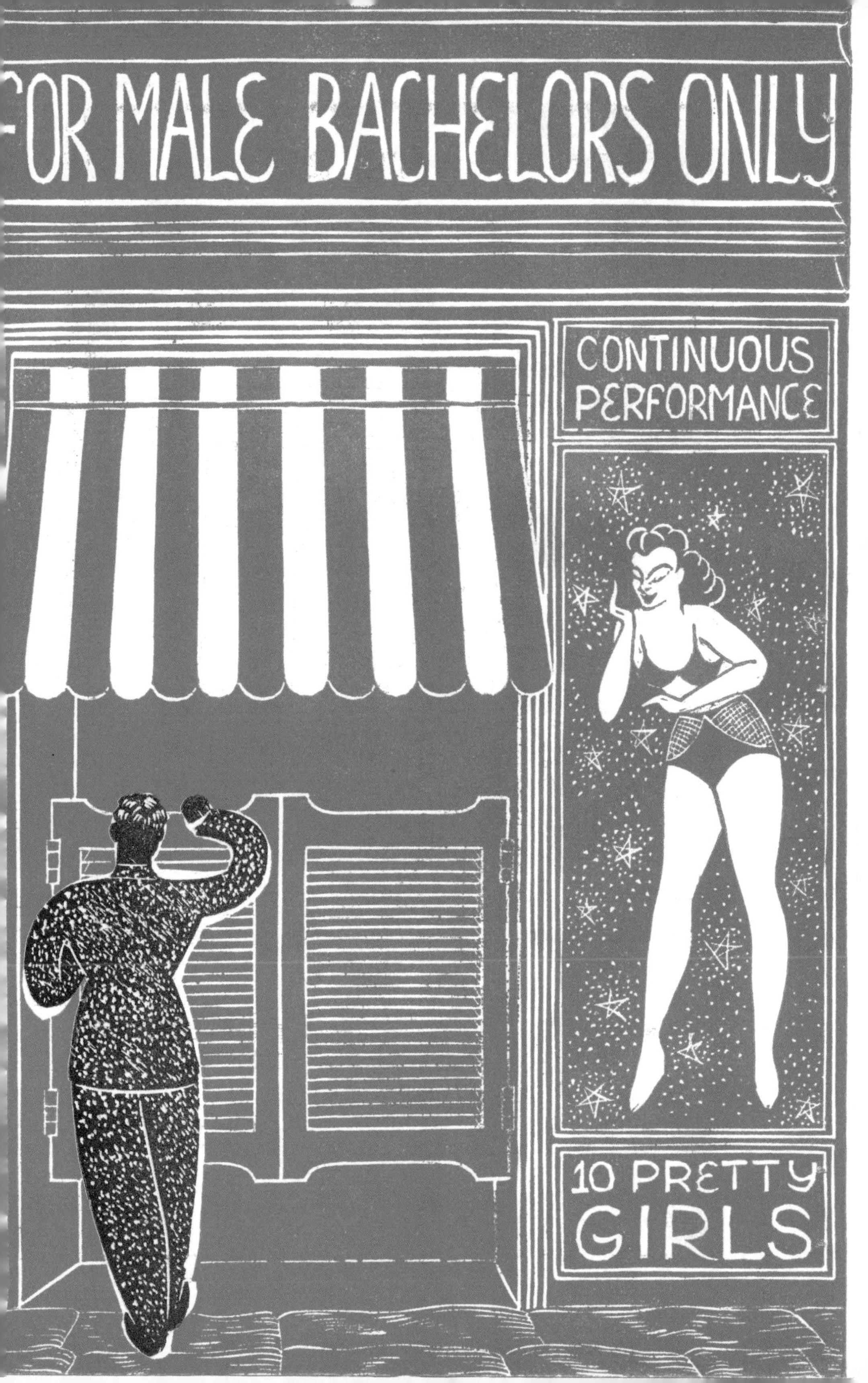
FOR MALE BACHELORS ONLY
CONTINUOUS PERFORMANCE
10 PRETTY GIRLS

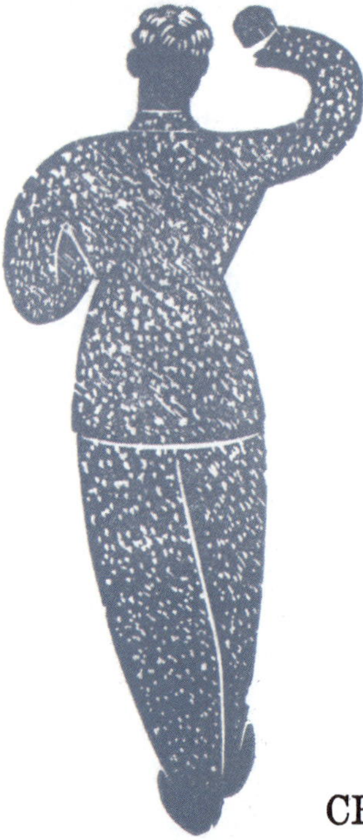

FOR MALE BACHELORS ONLY

CHAPTER FOUR

Unlike Rome, a good or rather a hearty Bachelor in New Orleans may take more than a day to burn—he may take a night or two. But gentlemen, you may wear asbestos underwear and a stone belt buckle, and yet burn quite up if you don't watch your cues.

In a certain quite dignified bar one afternoon recently, a young lady of apparent great dignity was sitting. She was an extremely well dressed brunette. From her voice, carriage, and manners, one would have deduced that she was a product of one of the better Eastern finishing schools.

Within fifteen minutes, she ordered and consumed with *great* nonchalance three straight Bourbon whiskeys. She smiled so charmingly at a middle-aged gentleman sitting next to her that he nearly fell off his bar stool. She glanced about the room, and then, noticing that a party of apparently well-heeled men, accompanied by but one female, had come into the bar and seated themselves at one of the tables, she slipped from her stool and sat down by herself at a table next to the party.

Within five minutes, she had introduced herself politely to that party and was a part of it.

There were four men in the party, it is important to remember. Since that afternoon, and the colorful, to say the least, evening that followed it, three of those men have lost, between them, in the neighborhood of fifteen thousand dollars. The fourth man, it seems, was pulled home by the ear by the woman who happened to be his wife and not the finishing-school-looking girl who was sitting at the bar.

Ah, well, that's life, of course—but how expensive!

That girl wasn't a prostitute, gentlemen, at least not in the accepted sense of the word. But it cost the three curious men an everage sum of five thousand bucks each before they finally admitted to themselves that the one thing they hadn't bought was what they had been paying for. Well, figure it out for yourselves.

A charming girl. You see her around the better bars frequently. She's probably head over heels in love with a floor-walker. Poor thing. But as for you, you might as well put fifty dollar gold pieces (if there are such things any more) into a coin derrick machine.

All of which points to some sort of moral. Which is, one supposes: If it glitters, it means gold.

At any rate, gentlemen, when in New Orleans, don't allow yourself to be picked up too easily, if you can help it, and if you are carrying too much money. Above all, don't try to make advances unless you can pretty well judge your opponent. If she is a nice girl or if she is happily married—or even unhappily, in most cases—you will probably get into all kinds of hell, and no doubt you will deserve it.

Taxi drivers, you will find, are gold mines of information. Some of them, of course, are not altruists in the least, and will lead you to places you may not, in the end, find comfortable. Beware of these: they can be identified by their too enthusiastic descriptions. If a cabby poetically pictures a night club to you that seems the dream of all good Bachelors, then the place is a dream, all right, but a nightmare. If, on the other hand, your cabby has an honest face and a bored voice, he probably is trustworthy.

If a cabby holds open his door to you and shouts happily: "Pretty girls! Pretty girls! Ten pretty girls!" turn around and run like hell.

In the first place, he is not telling the

truth: the girls are not pretty and there are not ten of them.

In the second place, there is something outrageously wrong: if he means what you think he means, that is, if he means what he says, then he is no doubt a ghost, for citizens of New Orleans, especially if they live uptown, assure us that the city has closed long since all such places.

If a young woman (or an old woman, for that matter) with whom you find yourself after a vague period of time says that she would like to "get out of all this," by all means sympathize with her, but let your feet be stirring as you do so. She means to say that she has notions of attaching herself to you and your pocketbook—if you have one left by this time—semi-permanently.

The reform of lovely ladies who need it has been tried by better men than you. The best you could hope for if you tried it would be an annual cuckolding by the deacon of your church. Give the Devil his due and treat him like a gentleman: don't try to work fancy tricks on him behind his back, for he doesn't like it. Who would?

But it all boils down to a simple final word of advice, gentlemen: always make friends platonically before you even think of making them anything else.

As for me, my windows already are broken.

★ ★ ★ ★ ★

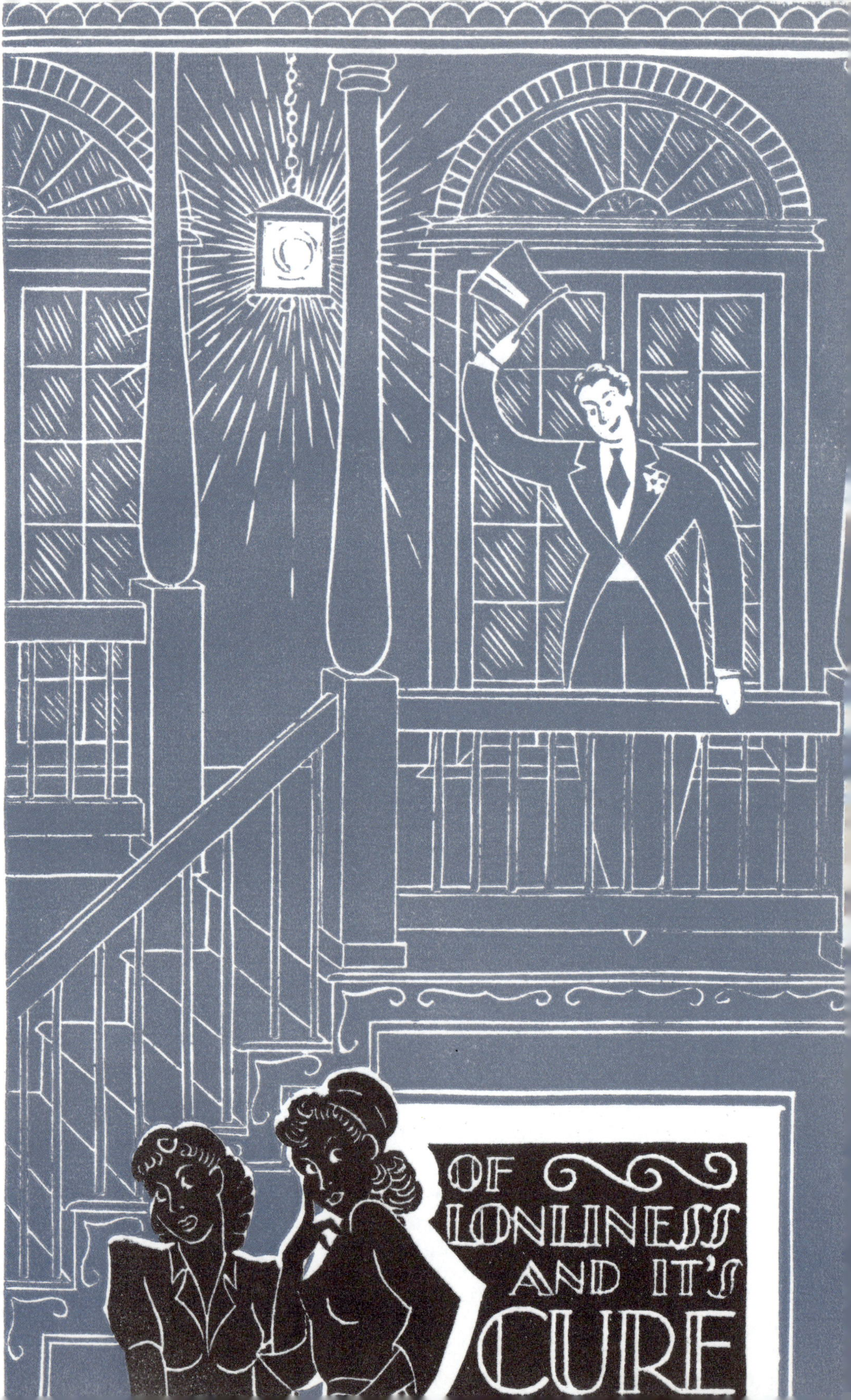
OF
LONLINESS
AND IT'S
CURE

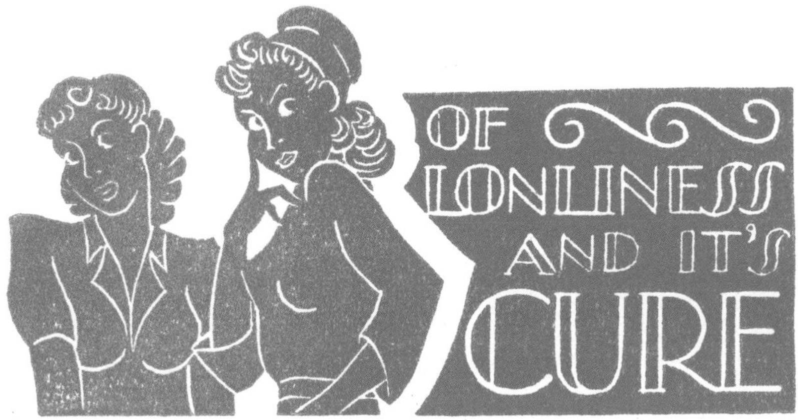

CHAPTER FIVE

It is bad enough to be lonely. To be lonely in New Orleans is, however, almost a merited punishment, for the feeling is easily banished.

Don't misunderstand. This is not a suggestion that you find any sort of paid escort or partner. In New York or Chicago, such a move might be necessary. Not in New Orleans.

A man or woman of even the weakest charm and the roughest good manners can, without fear of any embarrassment, go to almost any of the better New Orleans bars and within a short time, without effort, find him-or-herself acquainted with one or, more likely, several not unamusing people.

This is no chamber-of-commerce exaggeration. A spirit of genuinely informal friendliness prevails in New Orleans—particularly in the French Quarter of New Orleans. Anyone not a thorough dullard who has ever visited New Orleans for longer than five minutes can tell you so.

You go into a bar. You sit down and order a drink. You remain just as sedate and reserved as you like (within reason, of course). You muster a small amount of patience, if necessary—and it seldom is.

What happens?

The next morning when you wake you are the possessor of a speaking acquaintance with at least several people. That's putting it mildly, for the average case.

If you still are lonely, you need a doctor or a damned good love affair.[1]

The reason for the exceeding friendliness of the city probably lies in the fact that New Orleans is not, in the worst sense, a typical southern city, not a stronghold of militant southern regionalism. Professional New Orleanians can be found in plenty, but professional Confederates are less numerous than in, say, Atlanta, Richmond, or New York.

The French Quarter, particularly, is cosmopolitan. Here you meet Michiganians, Texans, New Yorkers, Virginians, Californians, Mississippians, Nebraskans, Alaskans, French, Spanish, Italians, Portugese, English, Irish, Scotch, Africans, Dutch, Germans, Fijiis, Mexicans, Chinese, Japanese, Belgians, New Zealanders, and so forth.

It makes no difference where you came from, what you did before you came here, or even how much money you have (that is, if you have enough to buy a few rounds of drinks!), just so you can say yes without

[1]In New Orleans are scores of good doctors, and also unlimited opportunities for a damned good love affair—but such matters are not within the scope of this book.

whispering and *give us another* without hesitating.

So why on earth be lonely? Why join correspondence clubs? Why talk to yourself? You're in New Orleans and you've hundreds of friends available. Loneliness eats at the heart and gnaws at the liver and divers other tender bits, but company quickly chases him away. Be a joy to your friends—but first, get some!

★ ★ ★ ★ ★

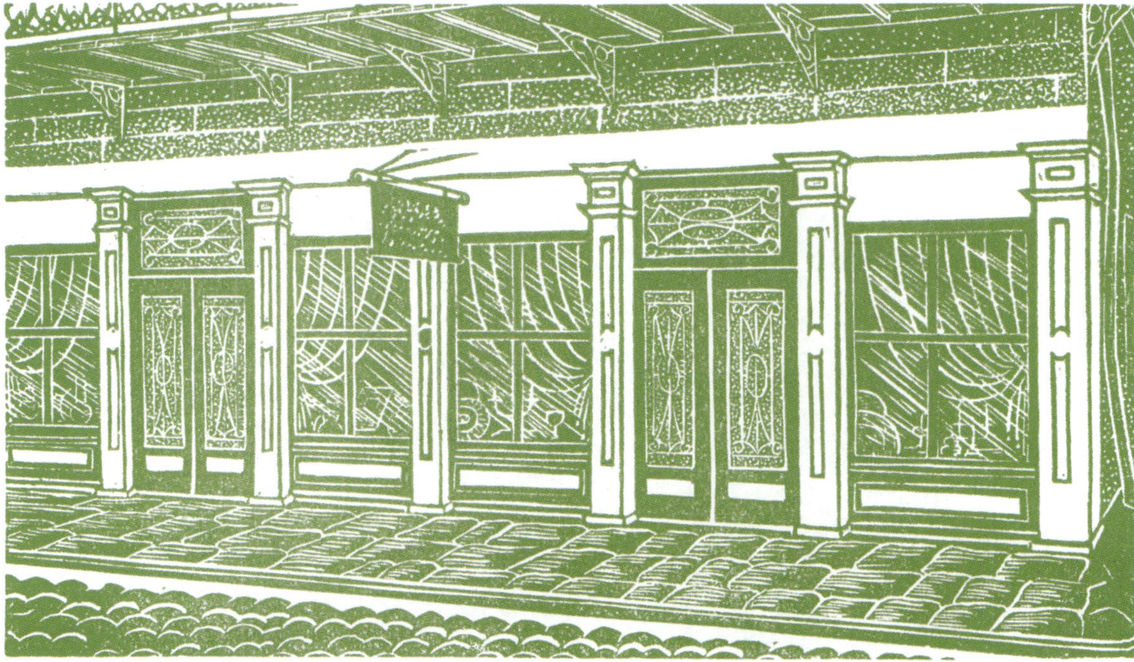

Chopin's Royal Gifts and Flowers

639 RUE ROYAL VIEUX CARRE NEW ORLEANS

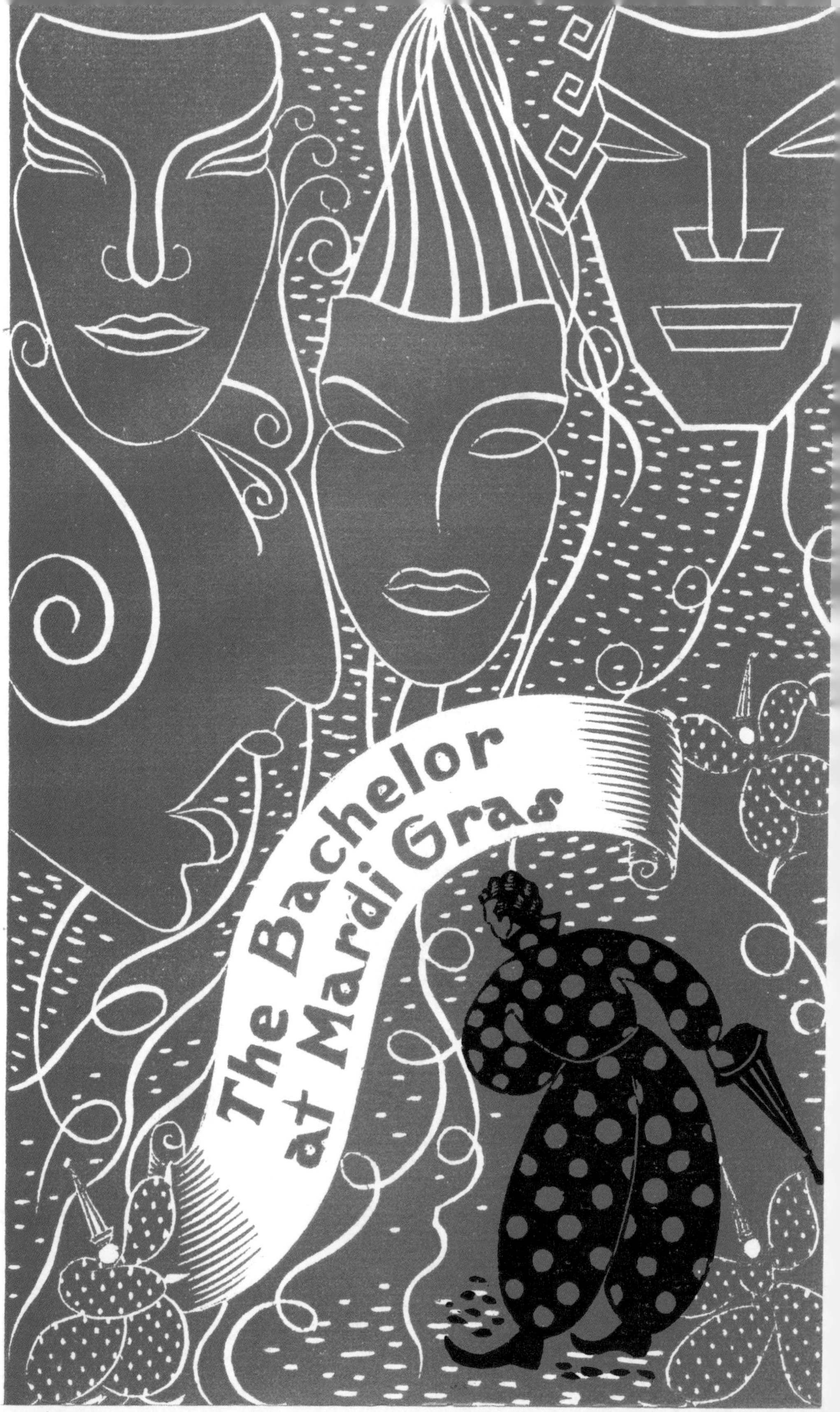
The Bachelor
at Mardi Gras

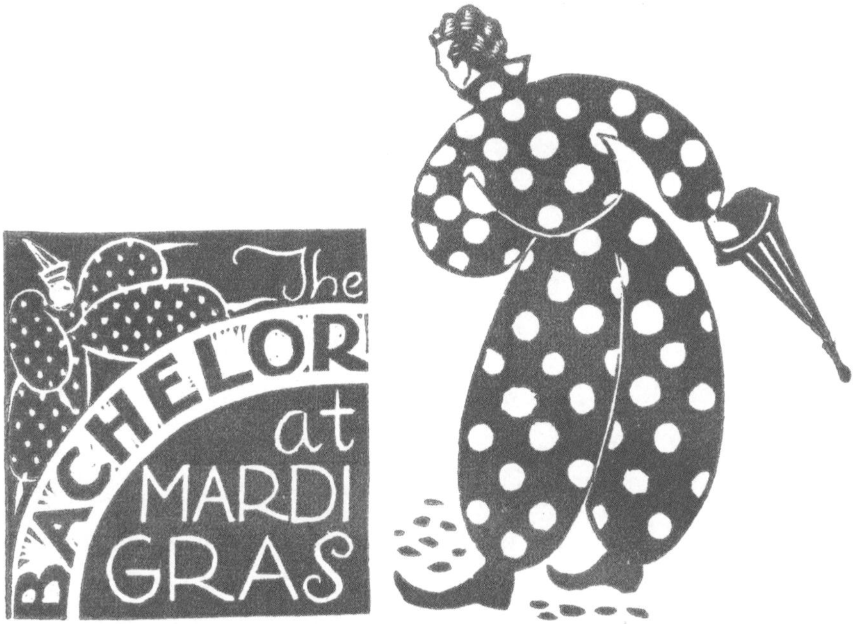

CHAPTER SIX

The following words will not serve well their purpose—for their purpose is to render the spirit of Mardi Gras accurately for those who have never been through one, and that is impossible.

You can't believe it, really. Every year in New Orleans, when about three weeks have passed since the year's birth, thus allowing for recovery from normal celebrations of the Christmas season, the citizenry begins to jam the bars. Exiled New Orleanians and veteran-survivors of former Mardi Gras periods begin to drift in from all over the world. A spirit (how flat that sounds, yet no other word can be used) begins to be noticeable all about. It is a gay spirit, a reckless, restless spirit, a spirit indescribably frolicsome.

The spirit gets you. You can't escape. You are walking along the street minding your own business and thinking well of yourself, when all of a sudden you find to your insincere horror that you have leapt into the air, clicked your heels together, and let out a resounding rebel yell!

You look down and find your feet performing a rapid dance as they move you straight for the nearest bar. Your dignity swoons dead away and you don't even bother to attend its funeral. You're off!

By the time you've paused in your laughter for a quick breath—that is, a week or so later—it is time for the parades to begin. You have been invited by this time to join a continuous party in an apartment in the French Quarter, and if you are fortunate, the apartment is on Royal Street and has a balcony.

You find yourself on a balcony, drink in hand, while below in the street crowds gather and a great hush falls. From afar, in the direction of Canal Street, there presently comes the sound of the laughter and cheering of a vast multitude. Horns—and not automobile horns—are blowing. Then you see it in the distance.

Hollywood has never produced such color in a spectacle. A million lights, a thousand flares, ten billion sequins and jewels mark the parade. Floats a quarter of a block long and so high some of the wires crossing the streets have to be taken down come slowly in a mile-long procession. Before each float walk proud Negroes carrying blazing flares, and when the bands play, these dusky attendants truck and dance. Horses prance beneath the trappings of princes and princesses of the parade societies. Great percherons majestically draw the giant floats. Beautiful women in incredibly luxurious costumes are everywhere in evidence. Crowned royalty of the societies toss favors to the dense crowds.

You grow dizzy from splendor witnessed, and you lose track of yourself.

For days and nights and nights and days this goes on unabated. Until finally Mardi Gras, the day before Ash Wednesday and Lent, arrives.

If you have survived the excitement of the build-up to Mardi Gras—and many hardy souls have passed on during this period—then the morning finds you in costume mingling with the seeming millions who pour unrestricted through the French Quarter Streets. Traffic in the Quarter is at a standstill, and even the police and the ministry are shouting. Practically everyone is in costume. You meet friends dressed as elks, mice, roaches, elephants, lions, tigers, snakes, skeletons, pirates, bums, sailors, shady ladies, monks, apples, cocktails, bottles of whiskey, strawmen, shoes, hangovers, and so forth. By afternoon you are convinced of nothing whatsoever save that the world has gone crazy and that you are damned glad of it.

There is something awe-inspiring about the spectacle of a whole city, and New Orleans is huge, on a spree, a real, honest-to-God, shouting, yelling, cavorting, hissy of a spree!

It is something you'll remember forever —vividly!

The next day is Ash Wednesday. Even if you aren't religious you'll know it's Ash Wednesday as soon as you wake. It is time to quit for a while, time to repent. It is time to cover your head with blessed ashes and to go forth in sackcloth. It is time to return to yourself and take stock.

The streets are curiously empty when you finally summon enough courage to take you outdoors. The few people you meet avoid your eyes and tend to speak in a whisper. Even the newsboys are subdued.

It's a good day to go to church, even though you belong to no church. At the Cathedral on Jackson Square the Mass is comforting. You have been a bad lad, but so has everyone in New Orleans, practically. Here you will find the saddened sinners not outnumbered by the righteous. It is the same in all New Orleans churches on this day. Contrite hearts are bleeding. Amen.

After church, if you go, it might not hurt to have one, one, just one, or *perhaps* two, in closest congenial bar.

With a drink or so in you, you will begin to feel better, possibly. Not unrepentant, of course, but *better, healthier*. Then you can shake your head and say "Never again—until next Mardi Gras!"

★ ★ ★ ★ ★

★ ★ ★ ★ ★

NOTE—The sad news has been received that Mardi Gras Carnival Societies have called off all parades, balls, and celebrations for this year (1942) and each succeeding year until the war is over.

There is weeping and wailing among faithful celebrants, but it is generally acknowledged that in these dangerous times it is best.

But very shortly Carnival will be King in New Orleans again. And, meanwhile, parades or no parades, balls or no balls, official celebrations or no—the spirit of Carnival will be wafting about in the days before Lent. Take a deep breath. . . . .

★ ★ ★ ★ ★

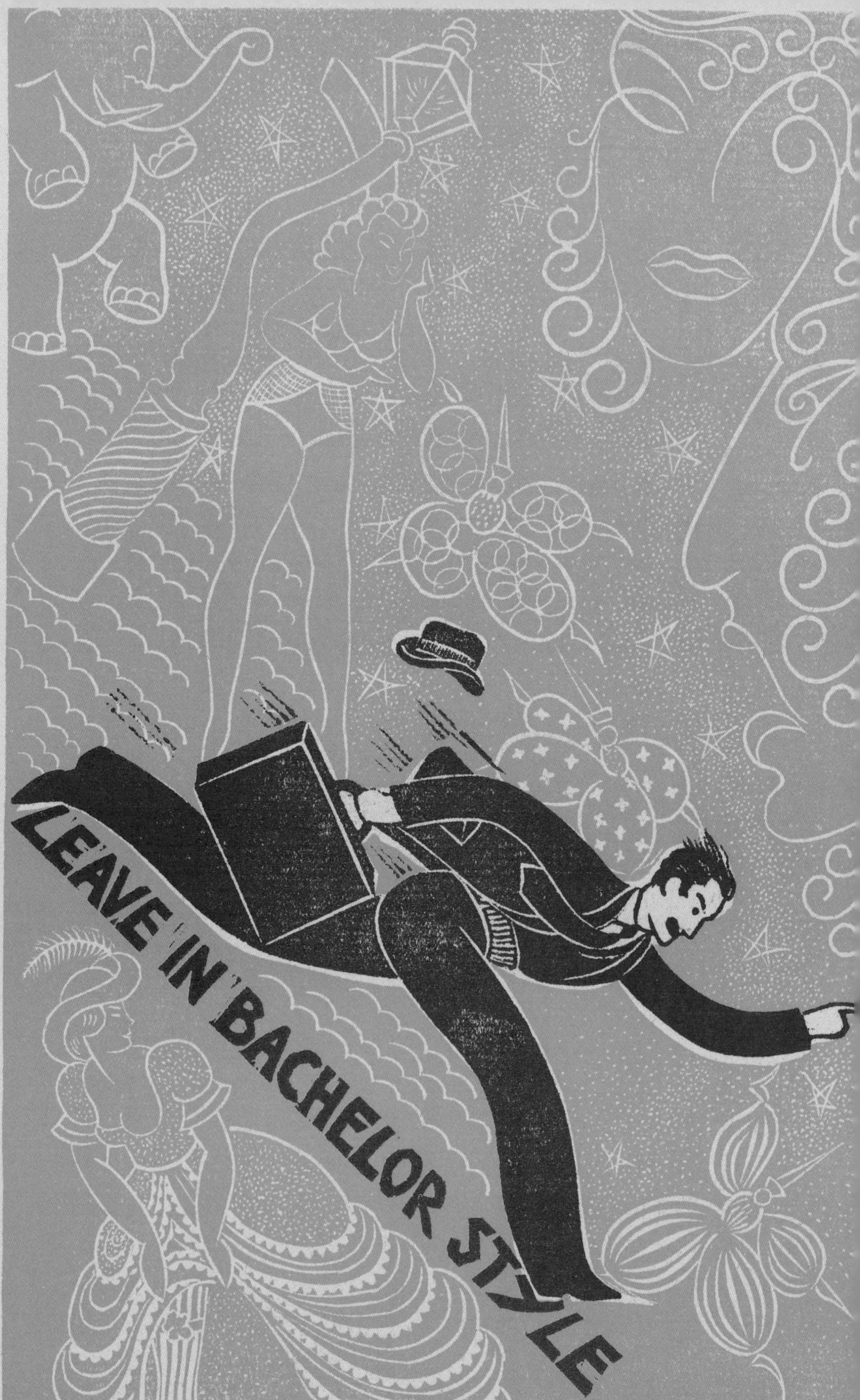
LEAVE IN BACHELOR STYLE

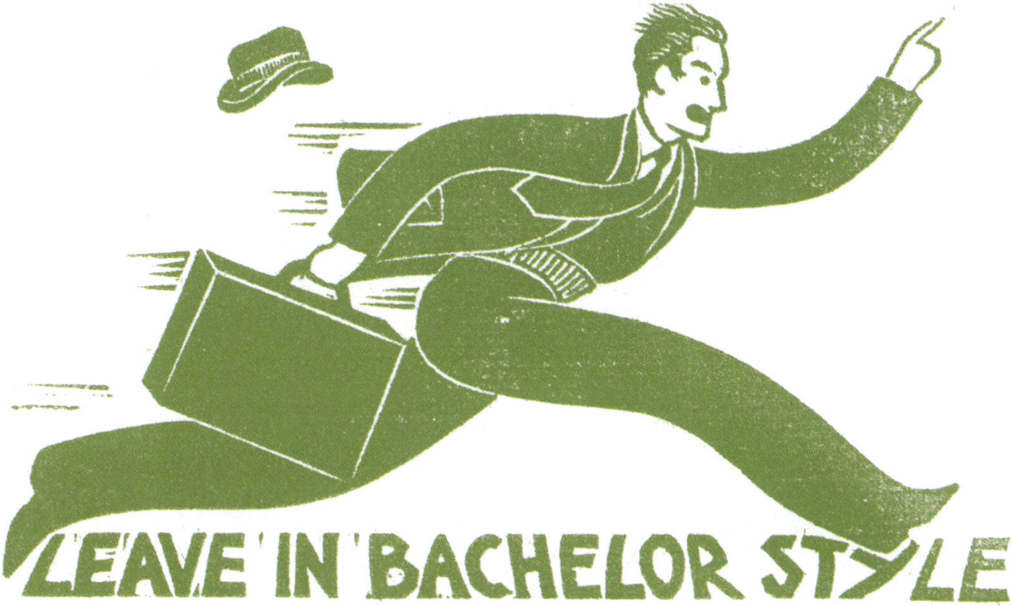

CHAPTER SEVEN

If you want to leave New Orleans in true Bachelor style, arrange your affairs and your schedule in such a way that it is possible for you to take a night plane, train, bus, or freight-car. The morning before you leave will be fearful enough without having to cope with bags, porters, tickets, and your own regretful heart. Besides, it is unwise to start off on a morning journey drunk: and try though you may, you'll never get out of New Orleans quite sober! At night, few will notice your unsteady step, your goofy smile, and such as are awake are likely to be fellow Bachelors in your own unrepentant condition. In the morning, people tend to stare at a celebrant. To be stared at dulls one's precious edge.

You have, of course, let all the friends you've made know that you are leaving. If you haven't told them, they know it anyway. There's a certain unhappy gleam in the eye of any Bachelor who is on the verge of leaving New Orleans. But at any rate, they are aware, and, being aware, are determined to send you off. You are due to be launched, so to speak.

Your telephone rings early the morning of your scheduled departure. Someone is in the Roosevelt or St. Charles or some other fine bar already beloved in your memory. Someone wants to tell you goodbye. Someone wants to buy you a farewell drink.

You are cautious. There is a decisive day ahead of you, a day fraught with the care of packing. There are telegrams to send, lies to manufacture for out-of-New Orleans consumption, ladies or gentlemen (well, you once thought they were ladies or gentlemen) to avoid, and so forth.

But just one farewell drink, your caller wheedles, you may never see him or her again.

You next are sitting at a table or perched at a bar and to your dismay you are having a wonderful time on three drinks and an empty stomach. Food is in order.

Your friend has multiplied to several by now. These folks, whom you have come to love like your own family by this time, assure you they'll fix you right up with some food. They consult with each other and then with the bartender.

Before you is placed a suspicious looking glassful of assorted things ordinarily strangers to each other. You make out an egg. You smell whiskey. Pepper makes your eyes water. A dark fluid is present, which you identify shortly as Worcester Sauce. There is salt in evidence.

You turn hurt eyes upon your friends. Oh, they ate long ago. But this is a traditional farewell breakfast for a Bachelor in New Orleans. Are you a mouse? or a Bachelor in New Orleans?

Your ancestors prepare to turn over in their graves in case you prove a coward in the face of this challenge. What would great-grandfather Adamantine have done, you ask yourself. With a sinking feeling, you are forced to confess that he would promptly have tossed the concoction down—just as you must do, so as not to shame him.

You learn just before you drink it that the stuff in your glass is called a depth bomb. As soon as you toss it down, you know why. You feel distinctly torpedoed!

Five minutes later you feel so good you could almost recommend that Hitler be hanged instead of broiled over a slow fire.

That is only the beginning, of course. By nightfall, you are, well, you are in what politely may be termed the condition of a Bachelor who is saying farewell to New Orleans. You, sir, are fried. Period.

You will insist, of course, being at heart a hospitable soul, that everyone you meet board the train with you and go home and share your roof for an unlimited space of time. Being charitable, you will attempt to give away your neckties and union suits to grinning bell boys. You will offer to buy the Huey Long Bridge, and it will seem to you highly necessary that you hire Antoine's best chef away from him. If you get on a plane, you will tell the hostess that you are going to speak to Goldwyn about getting her Hedy Lamarr's job. If you get on a train, you will tell the plump old lady into whose berth you climb by mistake that you represent the Twitchum Public Survey Associates and wish to know her considered opinion on the situation in the Far East. If you board a bus, you will inform the little Creole girl on your left, in a carefully lowered voice, that you are the Crown Prince of Merovingia travelling incognito. If you are travelling in a box car, you will inform your fellow hoboes, if they will listen to you, that if it hadn't been for that blonde. Oh, well, in short, you will have an irresistable impulse to spread some rather flattering but slightly misleading gossip about yourself.

By the time you are ten miles out of town you will have discovered and opened the pint that some friend has given you to tide you over the trip. Less than half of it should do the trick. When you wake up several hundred miles further on, you will be thinking utterly selfish thoughts.

It may be a month after this before it hits you bad. It may even be as long as six weeks. But there will come one day a sudden sharp pain. You will be walking down the street and a perfume will start it, perhaps, or the smell of fresh grass, or the sight of a quaint old rooftop silhouetted against a very blue sky, or pigeons may rise from the street in front of you, setting your memory fluttering like their wings. *New Orleans,* you will think, *New Orleans. . . . .*

The hurt of being away from New Orleans is like a sudden memory of some beautiful woman who once granted you her favors. It rises up in your throat and chokes you with nostalgia. It is a longing no words can express. New Orleans is the lotus land, to which all travellers return—once visited, it haunts you, calling your blood always.

To recapture past happiness in New Orleans, exiled Bachelors have some little tricks. They are not cures for the nostaglia, however, but merely medicines to ease it. There are no cures.

These Bachelors have been wise. With them from New Orleans they have brought ample supplies of such liquors as *Herbsaint*, *Liqueur d'Elite*, Peychaud Bitters (a delightful and time-tested ingredient for Sazeracs, old-fashioneds, gin fizzes, etc.), and Louisiana orange wine, and the necessary spices, seasonings, etc., for New Orleans cooking.

On nights when the longing for New Orleans becomes unbearable and it still is not possible for them to return, these Bachelors hie them to their kitchens, where they concoct New Orleans drinks, and after tossing these down with happy tears, set about preparing dinners of New Orleans dishes. (They have, of course, prepared themselves beforehand with New Orleans drink guides and cook books.)

It therefore is best for the Bachelor in New Orleans to prepare himself for such evenings before leaving the city. There are many stores and shops, of course, where a complete list of New Orleans liquors, seasonings, and even canned specialties such as shrimp gumbo and crayfish bisque can be obtained. But Solari's, at the corner of Royal and St. Louis Streets, is one of the most remarkable stores south of New York. Dealing entirely in fine and rare food and liquor specialties, Solari's is a *must* for the Bachelor who wishes to take something of New Orleans with him when and if he leaves.

★ ★ ★ ★ ★

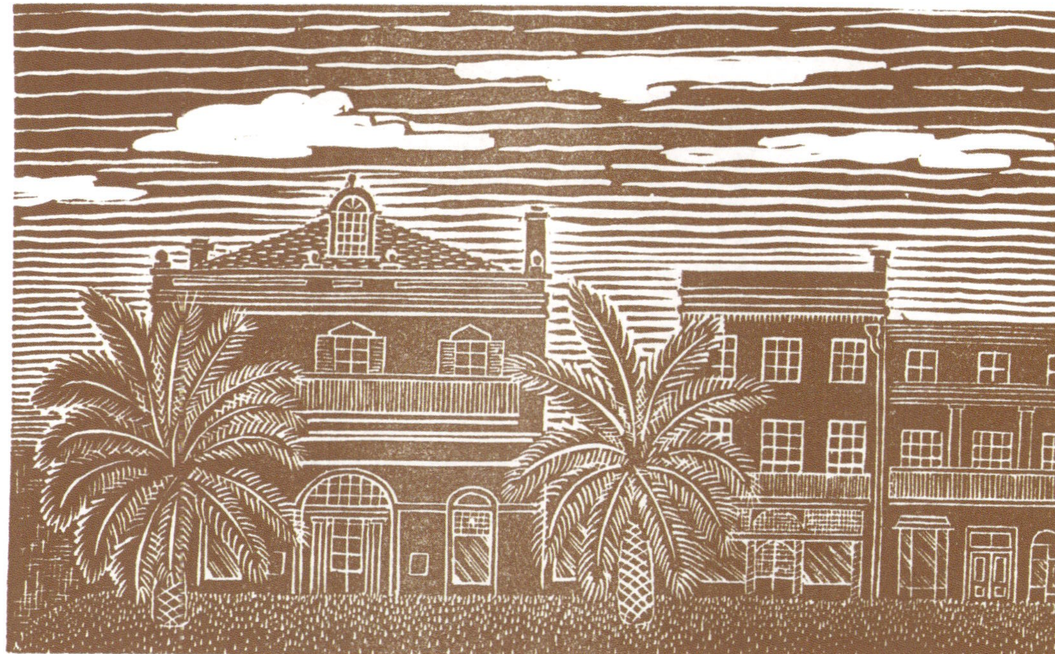

Louisiana State Bank Building—1819. Conti and Royal Streets

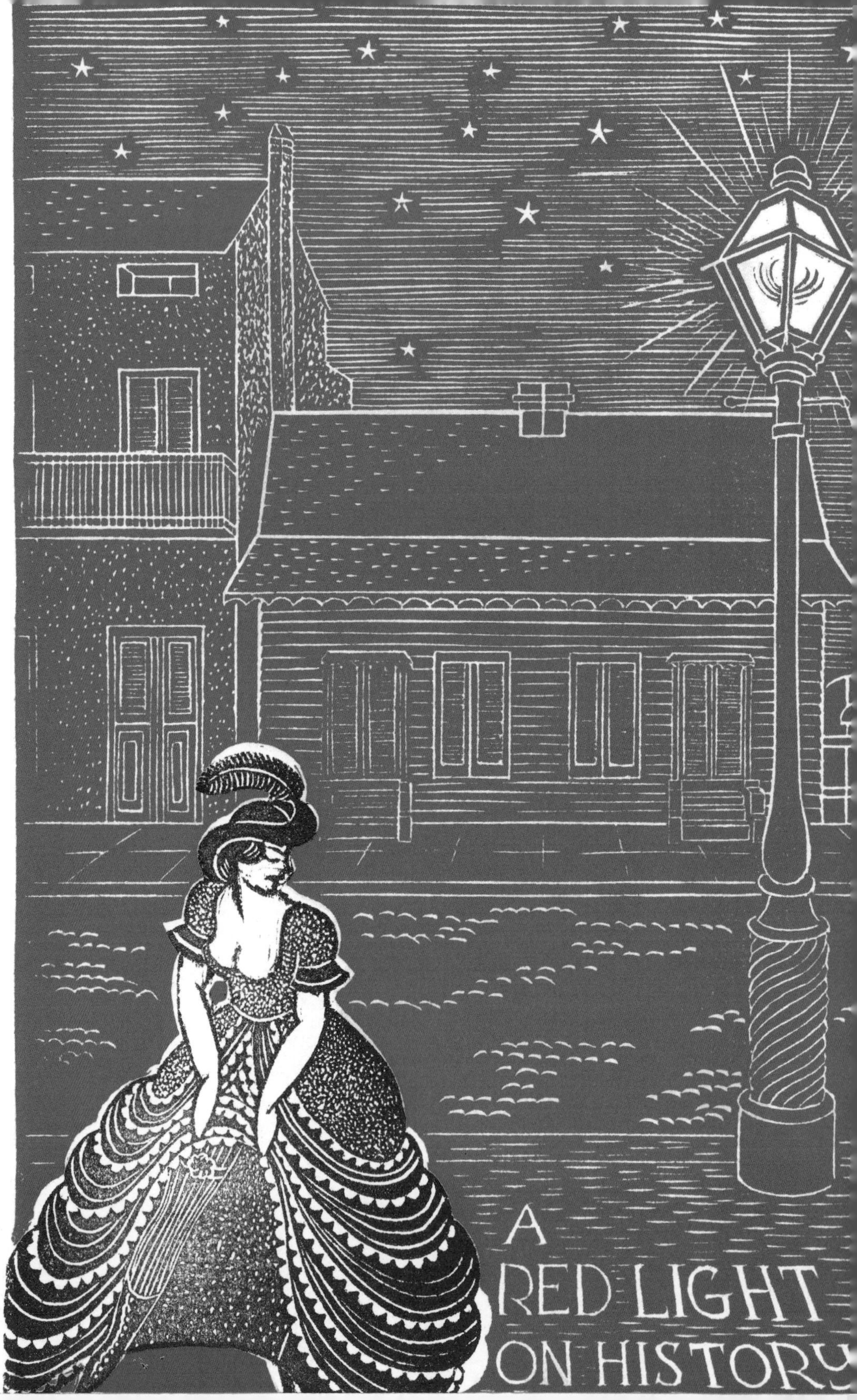
A
RED LIGHT
ON HISTORY

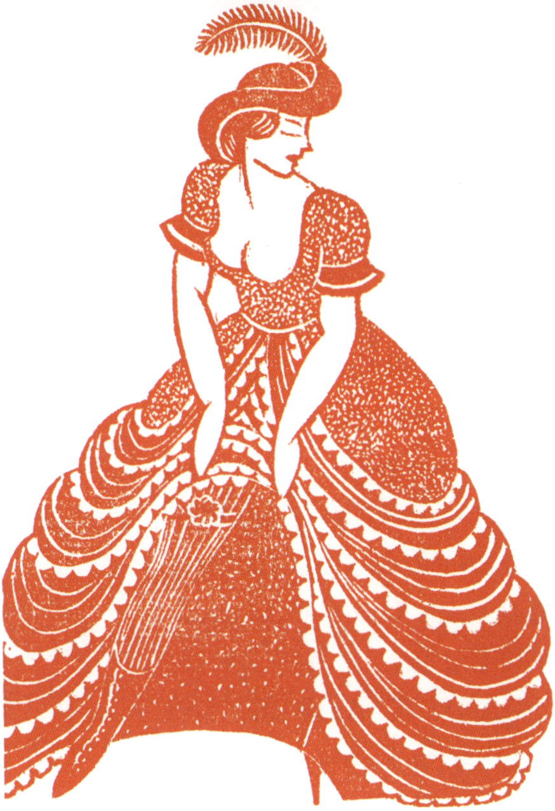

A RED LIGHT ON HISTORY

CHAPTER EIGHT

No other American city, not even San Francisco with its Barbary Coast, has enjoyed—and the word is used advisedly—such a vivid history of sin as New Orleans. Furthermore, the history was not ended until comparatively recent times. Many there are still in New Orleans who can recall the days when it was not uncommon to see prostitutes who carried their bedding under their arms while they solicited and carried on "business" on sidewalks or parkings.

Other cities notorious for scarlet happenings have had decades of wideopen vice—New Orleans has had a decade or two, recently, of comparative respectability. As late as the turn of the century, New Orleans houses of prostitution were so popular and so well accepted by the citizenry at large that guidebooks and newspapers devoted to their life and interests still were being published. The society column of the *Sunday Sun*, for instance, was called SCARLET WORLD, and was made up of "Interesting Items About the Everyday Life of Women of Crimson Circles." In this column for January 31, 1904, New Orleanians were informed that Miss Josie Arlington was "suffering with a bad cold," but that she was "on deck all the same attending to business." On the same day, the columnist wrote, "Tillie Thurman . . . . is certainly a Pelican of the first water. Boys, if you are out looking for a good time and wish to save a doctor's bill we severely advise you to give the above establishment all the room possible." And Winchell was only a pup in 1904!

Grand scale prostitution in New Orleans began shortly after the Louisiana Purchase, early in the nineteenth century. Women were so cheap that they could be purchased, with drink and a night's lodging, for as low as a picayune, as the six-cent piece was then called. Lawlessness was so complete that in one district, known as the Swamp, a policeman was not seen for twenty years. This district remained notorious for its population of thieves, cheap prostitutes, and human derelicts for nearly a century.

It was not until the boom of the eighteen-thirties, however, that the famous luxury-houses of New Orleans became numerous. A few dignified and discreetly operated houses had existed before this time in the French Quarter, but they were in the European tradition and are not to be compared with the peculiarly American luxury bawdy houses that were to spring up so noisily in New Orleans. By 1850, the latter type of house of prostitution was becoming well established in the city, and the ladies of pleasure were by that time resident outside the underworld sections. They spread into the fine residential districts like germs into healthy tissue, and a city government spectacularly corrupt in the best rugged individualist manner did little or nothing to discourage them.

By 1870, it is said, there were very few blocks indeed in New Orleans without at least one "sporting house".

Politicians and police received excellent pay in those days, for, besides their official salaries, they received tribute from the bordels. The politicians collected through agents. Policemen nightly collected from the front steps of the houses piles of silver left there by the women who inhabited them.

As business in flesh boomed, one New Orleans street more than any other perhaps in the world achieved a reputation for the number and the abandon of its houses of pleasure. Though its name now has been changed by a blushing city to Elk Place, in one section, and Crozat Street, in another, Basin Street, subject of the famous *Basin Street*

Blues, still is well remembered.

After 1880, Basin Street was one solid river of vice. Both sides were lined with bordels of incredible splendor, furnished with all the elegance that unlimited money and bad taste could achieve.

One of the first of these, Kate Townsend's, erected in 1866 on the site of the present Elk's Club, seems to have enjoyed some social distinction. In an article in the New Orleans *Times* for September 22, 1870, a writer signing himself "Suffering Property Holder" stated that Kate Townsend's sporting house was built with contributions from a high police official, a Recorder, and some of the members of the Common Council. The writer said, "Indeed, we have understood that the lady of an Alderman . . . . resolved to see for herself. She disguised herself and entered the house, where she found nearly the whole city government. . . . ."

Other Basin Street "sporting palaces" followed Kate Townsend's, and many were even more magnificent. Some of the more famous were Minnie Haha's (Minnie claimed to be descended from Hiawatha's sweetheart in Longfellow's poem!); Leila Barton's; Gentle Annie Reed's—later Kitty Johnson's; Josephine Kileen's—where one of the "girls" sold not only herself but her ten year-old daughter for a lump fee of fifty dollars per night; Kate Smith's near Canal Street—which advertised that its girls were all seventeen or under; Hattie Strauss' three story house known as Twenty-one; and Fanny Sweet's.

The less elegant houses flourished no less in the last half of the Nineteenth century. Enjoying such appetizing titles as Pig-Trough Carrie's, a twenty-five cent crib-house, the Picayune House, and McCarty's Ranch, these more democratic establishments made their profit on volume trade.

Also flourishing was the street-walking business in these times. Dauphine Street, in the French Quarter, was particularly rowdy. Sidewalk prostitutes unrolled their rugs for a dime, while in the cribs ladies could be purchased for as little as fifteen cents—cash.

A spectacular character in these days was a gentleman known as Joe the Whipper, who operated on Dauphine and Burgundy Streets. Joe was a familiar figure, and carried in his black bag a full assortment of whips, rods, switches and other instruments of torture for the use of which he was paid by prostitutes whose appetites were somewhat jaded by garden-variety excitements. Joe's sweetheart was a lady of color named Red Light Liz who worked in an establishment at 111 Dauphine Street.

On Burgundy, between Bienville and Conti Streets, was a district called Smoky Row, where reigned four holy terrors of bawdrydom, Fighting Mary, Kidney-Foot Jenny, One-Eyed Sal, and Gallus Lou, ladies of color, renowned, as their names imply, for their horrible skill in fighting. In this district, the random stroller was not invited inside a prostitute's room: he was dragged by the sleeve or collar, or, if he resisted successfully, his hat was obtained in order to bait him inside.

In 1891, the New Orleans police department proposed the enactment of a law providing for the compulsory medical examination of "all women and girls notoriously abandoned to lewdness," but this came to nothing. The virtuous ladies of New Orleans, at a mass meeting, defined this suggestion as an insult to Southern womanhood!

In 1877, the district that was to become known as Storyville, and as such incredibly infamous, was set aside by law for the dwelling and operating place of prostitutes, and they were forbidden to live or do business in any other part of New Orleans. Originally, the ordinance called for two areas of segragation, one above Canal Street, in the American section, and one below, in the French Quarter, but for some unknown reason, the French Quarter area appears to have been the only one inhabited generally by the ladies of pleasure.

It was here, in Storyville's houses of prostitution, that jazz was born. One of the famous octoroon houses, Lulu White's Mahogany Hall, is celebrated in the great jazz piece, the Mahogany Hall Stomp, popularized decades ago by Louie Armstrong. The Spasm Band, called by many authorities the first American jazz group, played often for the entertainment of the patrons of Storyville brothels. Besides Louie Armstrong, many another famous jazz musician of today got his start playing in Storyville.

Storyville continued in full and magnificent sway until October 1917, when Mayor Martin Behrman reluctantly bowed to the orders of the War and Navy Departments and introduced an ordinance in the City Council providing for the eradication of the district.

Within a short time, the prostitutes had vanished from Storyville. Thinking that they now would lack the means of making a living, women prominent in church work met with members of the Louisiana Federation of Women's Clubs and appointed a committee to give aid to the exiled Storyvillagers. Apparently, however, few needed their help, for the shady ladies had moved to other parts of New

Orleans, including the better residential districts, and were doing a good enough business.

After the war, however, prostitution in New Orleans took a turn for the worse. The good old days were over.

Ah, well, it was big, bad, and bold—while it lasted.

★ ★ ★ ★ ★

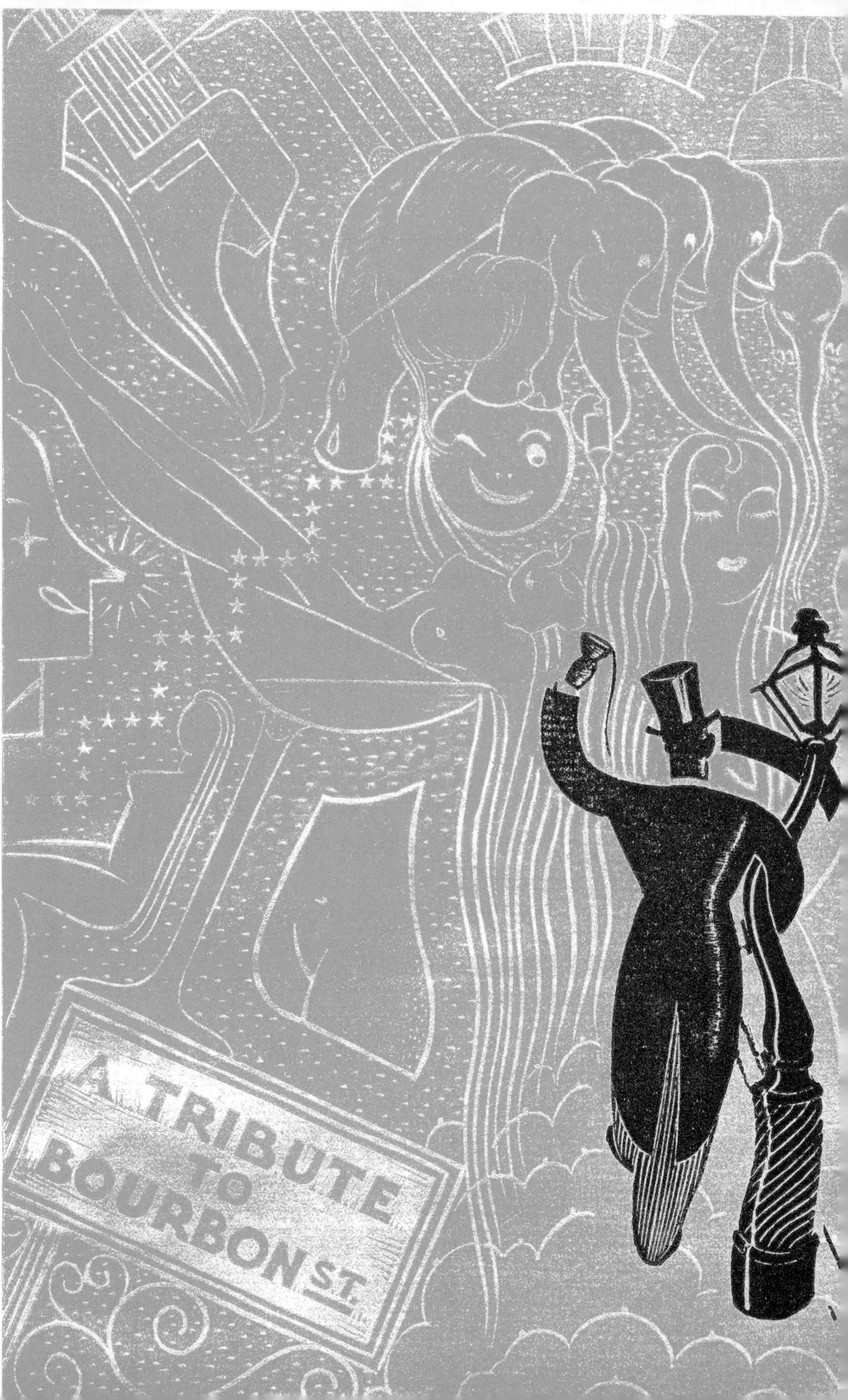
A TRIBUTE TO BOURBON ST.

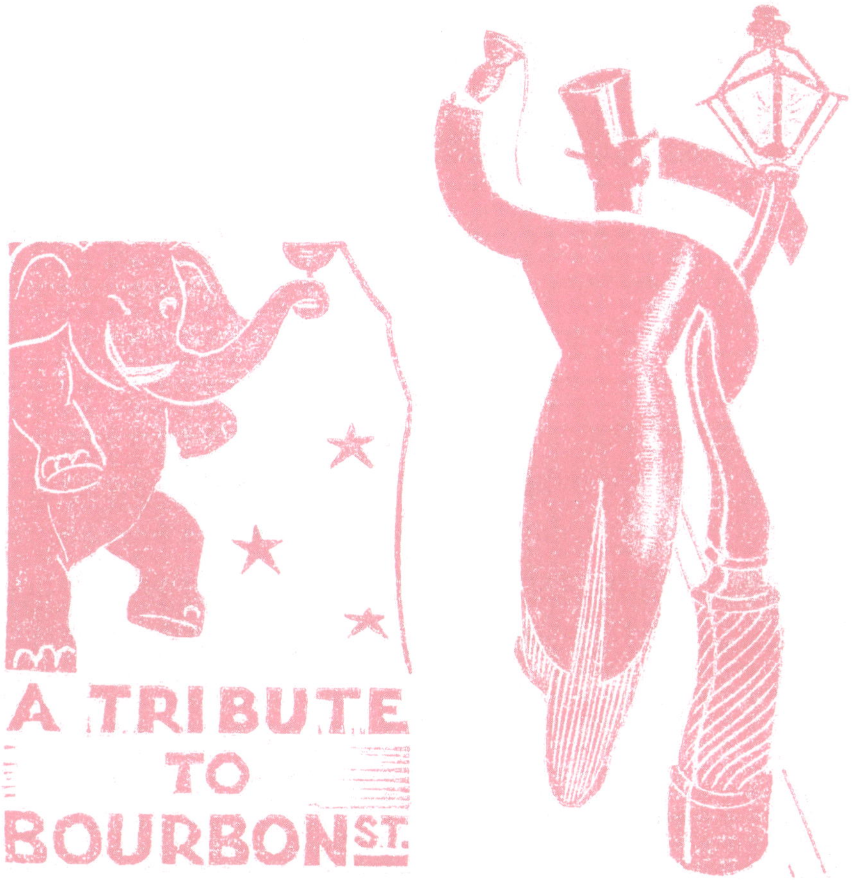

CHAPTER NINE

Bourbon Street, for the purposes of the Bachelor in New Orleans, is a channel of diversions extending through the French Quarter from Canal, the head, to Esplanade, the foot.

Bourbon Street is a place of scores of all-night clubs, large and small, clubs specializing in purely Bachelor entertainment. In appearance no gay White Way, this street yet is to New Orleans what Broadway is to New York. Here are honkey-tonks and gilt-and-silver supper clubs; here are clubs with "B-girls"[1] by the score and clubs with strip-tease entertainers; here are floorshows with dozens of lovely dollies and floorshows with a few boney old hags grinning through their routines in horrible travesty; here is the gamut of night life.

At any time of the day or night, the Bachelor can find something doing on upper Bourbon. What is doing may not be particularly pious, but it generally is educational. To see three generations of B-girls—one of about seventeen, another of about thirty, and a third of perhaps fifty years—working the same bar at once is not uncommon. Fluffy, painted, willowy young men are to be seen here and there (though there are other sections where this dilemmatic type is more plentiful) in the

[1] The B-girl is a lady, frequently of purchasable virtue, who works up drinks with a percentage from the bar or club as her salary.

less reputable clubs. There are many lamentable and interesting sights.

The adventure- loving Bachelor in New Orleans would do well to set aside one night now and then for exploring Bourbon Street. On such a night, he will walk down Bourbon from Canal. When he has gone one block, he will be in honkey-tonk land. From every doorway faint or raucous sounds will reach his ears, interesting sounds. The sounds will be a blend of music from jazz bands, the shrill laughter of women, the rattling of cocktail shakers, the guffaws of slightly tight menfolk, and the husky complaining of torch-singers.

If the stoutest Bachelor were to take two drinks in every Bourbon Street spot in the first five blocks away from Canal, he would find himself carrying a beautiful load. (He probably would be carrying a bevy of blondes as well!) Or, if he tried to have one drink in every bar on Bourbon between Canal and Esplanade, it would be days before he reached that latter thoroughfare and months before he got back uptown.

So take it easy. Look in doorways (though the Bachelor must beware of being dragged inside by the doormen!) and listen to the sounds that trickle out. Select your night club or bar with some care, and then enter bravely with an open mind. Something —either pleasant or unpleasant, or both— should happen. If it doesn't, the place is experiencing a dull hour. Move on. Try another. Eventually you'll find an experience, a happening that should either broaden you or scare you somewhat. Keep one hand on your glass and the other on your hip pocket and all the buttons on your clothes—and you'll survive almost anything not extraordinary on Bourbon Street.

If you talk to any of the veteran entertainers in these spots, you'll find that beneath their cynical shells they are extremely sentimental about Bourbon Street. "There's no place like it," they'll tell you, "no place, Chicago, Kansas City, New York, no place at all. Here a party can live his own life and nobody cares."

It is then that you realize with a shock that these tough night workers feel the same way about New Orleans that young art students used to feel about Greenwich Village. They are living as they please down here, so they say: and most of us had always believed they did that wherever they were!

So perhaps they're right, these M.C.'s and B-girls and torch singers and chorus lads. There is, there must be, no place like Bourbon Street!

★ ★ ★ ★ ★

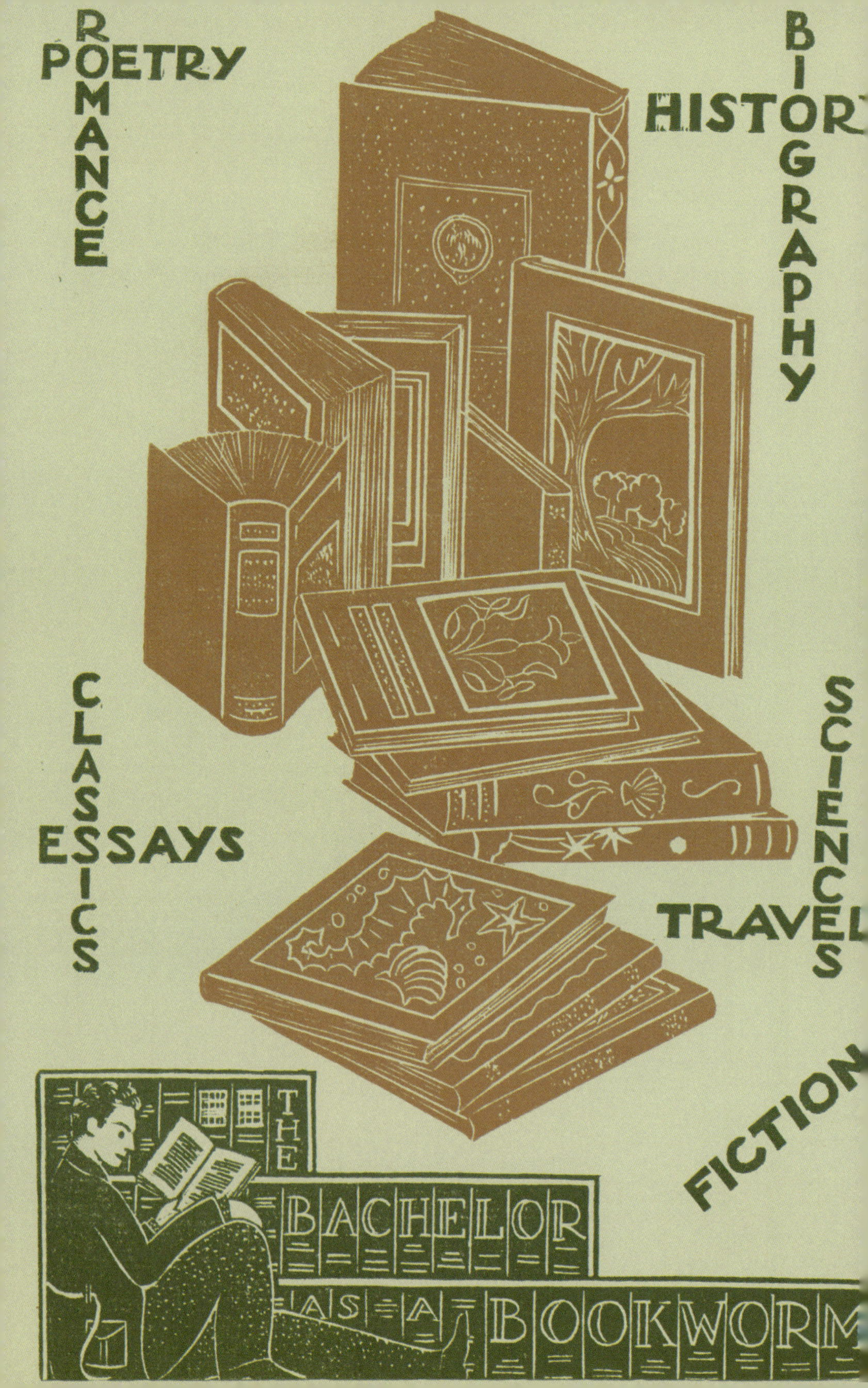
POETRY
ROMANCE
HISTORY
BIOGRAPHY
CLASSICS
ESSAYS
SCIENCES
TRAVEL
FICTION
THE BACHELOR AS A BOOKWORM

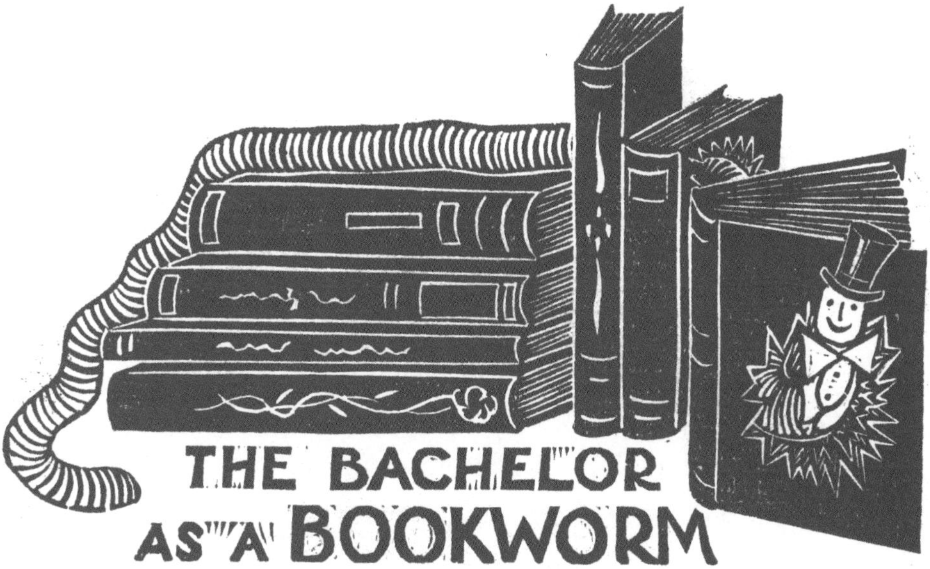

CHAPTER TEN

New Orleans has always been a city of Books, and many are the Bachelors in New Orleans who have written them. Some of the great who have lived here and worked here have left vivid stories of the New Orleans of the past. Many of the famous writers who have worked in New Orleans in recent years or who still are shattering lovely mornings with the thunder of their typewriters in the city have their names printed repeatedly in the best-seller lists.

One of the earliest writers to discover the charms of New Orleans for the creative personality was William Makepeace Thackery. Here Abraham Lincoln (and if you don't think he was a great writer, you haven't read his addresses!) came as a young backwoods trader, a raftsman, to wach and marvel at America's Queen City. A contemporary of Lincoln's, the poet Walt Whitman worked in New Orleans as a newspaper writer for a time. Audubon, scarcely less an author than an artist, roamed New Orleans' fascinating streets. Grace King and others made the city and its people material for their distinguished or popular writings.

Since the first World War, however, New Orleans has had its own renaissance of letters within the larger literary revival of the South. Sherwood Anderson forsook the comfort of a fat advertising income to dwell here, among other places, and write his nostalgic evocations of an America in confused transition. William Faulkner spent poverty-stricken but well-rewarding years in the French Quarter writing books that nobody then seemed to want (and how the publishers have fought over him since!). Roark Bradford and Lyle Saxon still make New Orleans their headquarters. E. P. (Pat) O'Donnell, of GREEN MARGINS and THE GREAT BIG DOORSTEP fame, reigns shyly in the French Quarter. Mary King, whose QUINCIE BOLLIVAR was the Houghton-Mifflin Fellowship Prize Novel of 1941, broods over a typewriter off Pirates Alley. Stanley Clisby Arthur has made New Orleans and Louisiana the subject of prodigious and much historical writing. There are many others . . . .

But for every literature-producing Bachelor in New Orleans there are hundreds of literature-consuming Bachelors. New Orleans is, fittingly, a place of book shops, circulating libraries, and sidewalk book peddlers.

In contrast to the large, well-stocked book shops above Canal Street are the old book shops of the French Quarter. At times, books are stacked and overflowing on the sidewalks before these quaint establishments, and the stroller has no choice but to pick his way through the volumes if he wishes to proceed. Some shops are dark and mysterious within. No one seems about. Absolute quiet reigns. You enquire of the shadows the price of a book. Five minutes later, if you are fortunate, an ancient scholar, book and glasses in hand and beard atilt, grumblingly shuffles from some haunted retreat in the rear. Chances are he dislikes selling books: it interferes with his own reading. If you plead with him, you may be able to buy the volume of your fancy. Or you may not. You may bear the brunt of a lengthy dissertation on the superior culture of the ancient Celts, or you may have to confess, lest you be promptly maimed, that it is highly probable that Bacon ghost-wrote Shakespeare. But your chances of being amused are somewhat better than your chances of violent death—and it's worth a chance!

★ ★ ★ ★ ★

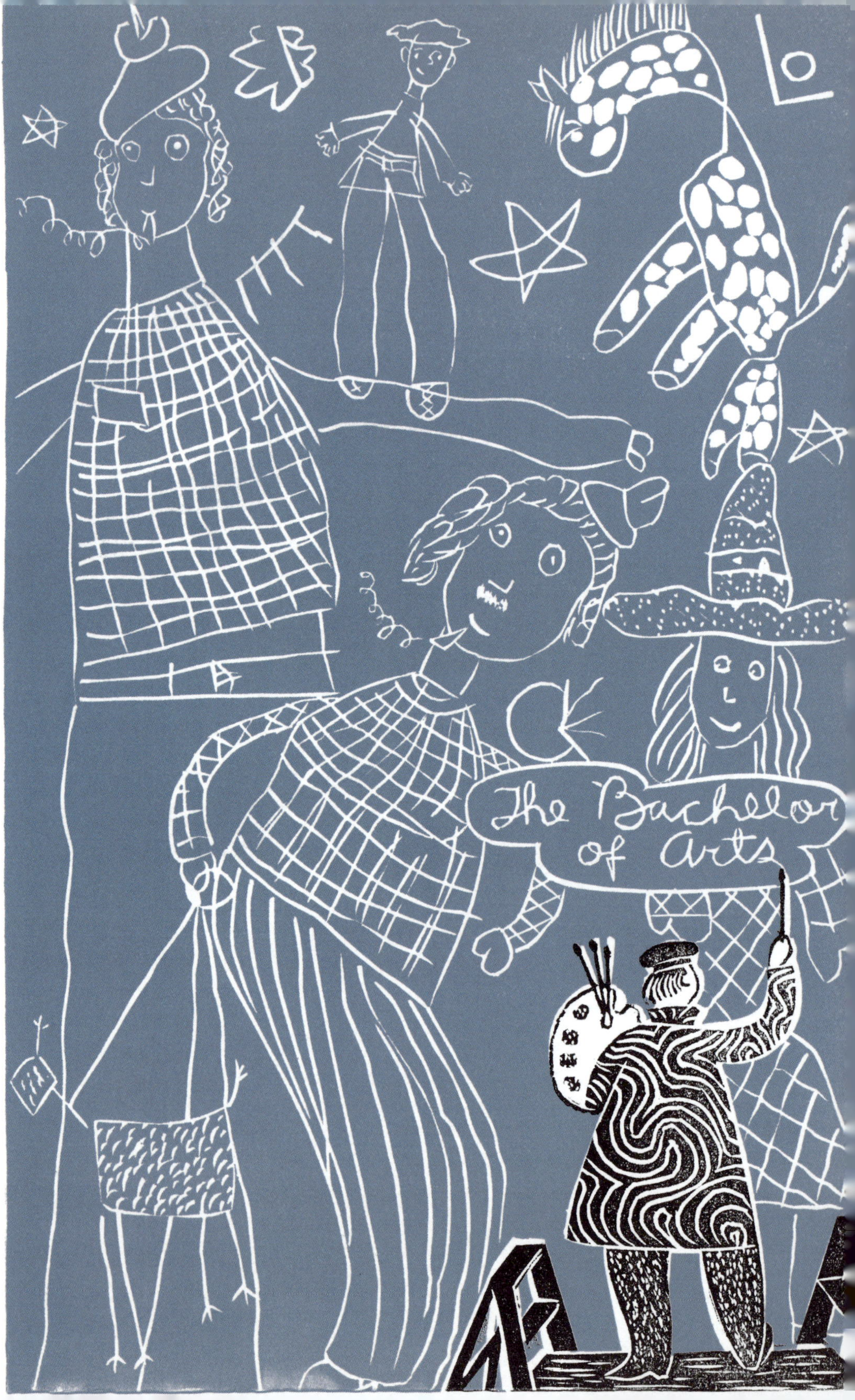
The Bachelor of Arts

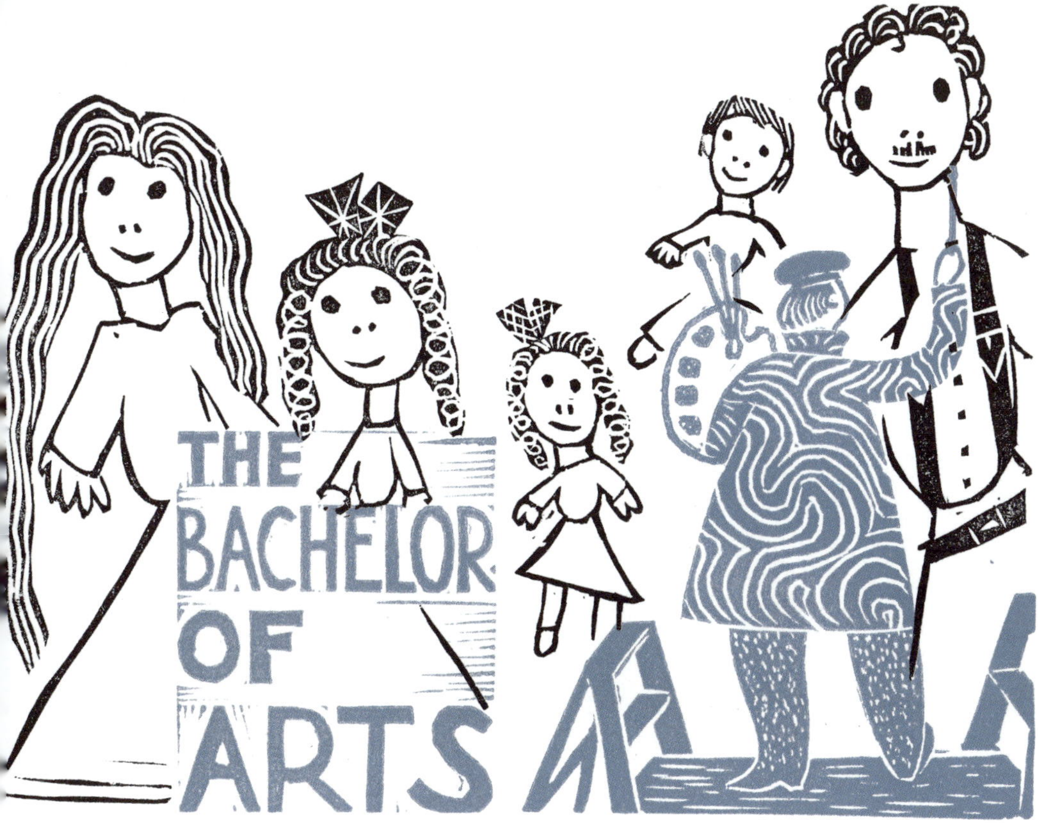

CHAPTER ELEVEN

There are Bachelors whose taste in art runs to the barroom nude and there halts out of breath. This chapter is not addressed to them. Most Bachelors, however, have a certain amount of curiosity about art—some even have respect for it. This interest Bachelors in New Orleans are able to pursue at leisure, for no other American city has more prolific artist inhabitants per square inch.

(The figures The Bachelor of Arts is painting were drawn by Lofrend, six-year-old-daughter of Eugenia and Bob Riley.)

There will come to each of you an afternoon when drink bores, theatres prove uninteresting, and none of the more routine diversions seems to invite you. You feel like nothing so much as a haphazard stroll. On such a day, a round of the art galleries and shops should prove just the thing. If you wish, you can see as many as several hundred interesting pictures in an afternoon.

There are not only the large public museums and galleries to visit. You are extremely welcome in the scores of small galleries and art shops. These establishments have paintings, etchings, drawings, bits of sculpture and so forth—for sale, of course; and though you are in no way committed to buy anything when you ask to look around, you may wish to pick up a painting, drawing, or piece of sculpture for your private collection or for a gift to a friend, a wife, a sweetheart, or an amorous or amorous-to-be acquaintance. (You'd be surprised what a well chosen landscape or etching—if you insist—will do for you where two dozen American

Beauty roses failed!)

The small art shops and galleries are located mainly in the French Quarter and most of them are to be found in the first nine or ten blocks of Royal Street from Canal Street. Many specialize in pictures and general art works, but almost all the book and gift shops have for sale as a side-line the works of local artists.

Among the most famous painters New Orleans claims from the past is John James Audubon, whose nature studies, particularly the "Birds of America" series, brought him a degree of immortality. Edgar Degas, the great French Artist, painted while in New Orleans in 1873 his famous "Cotton Factor's Office," valued today at more than $75,000. George Innes, the first American Impressionist painter, and Joseph Pennell, the great illustrator, also did work of importance while in New Orleans.

Today, however, the list of New Orleans artists who have won national attention is large. Particularly outstanding among these are Will Stevens, Xavier Gonzalez, Paul Ninas, Boyd Cruise, John McCrady, Virginia Parker, Olive Leonhart, Morris Henry Hobbs, and Dr. Marion Souchon, painters and etchers, and Enrique Alferez, Albert Rieker, and Angela Gregory, sculptors. A younger group of New Orleans painters and sculptors is producing work of great promise. Of these, Joseph Donaldson, Jr., a highly original watercolorist, and Carl Durel, a talented sculptor, already have gained considerable attention.

Alberta Kinsey and Knute Heldner are outstanding among the conservative artists of the Quarter.

At any rate, Bachelors, devote at least one afternoon to gallery trotting. And don't be afraid to laugh at the bad imitations of Picasso and Dali, *if* you're sure the artist isn't about. Pick your comedy, look about carefully for artists (and remember that the painters of surprisingly small pictures often are surprisingly husky guys!), and when the coast is clear, laugh like hell. Then assume a sober face quickly, and simply stare curiously at the round dozen artists who will appear from nowhere to see if it was their work someone was laughing at.

★ ★ ★ ★ ★

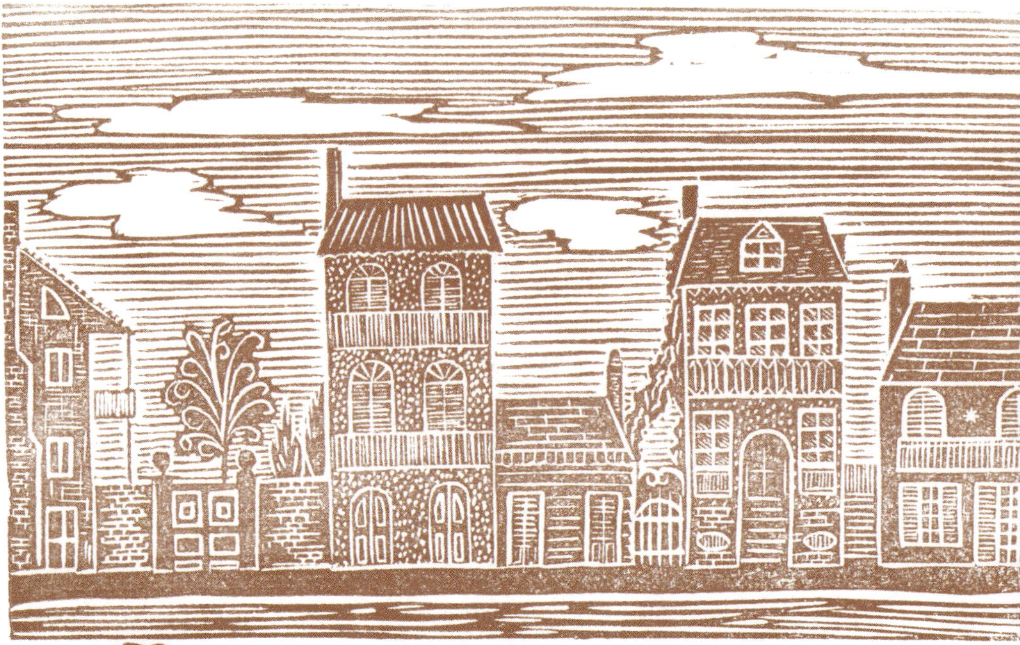

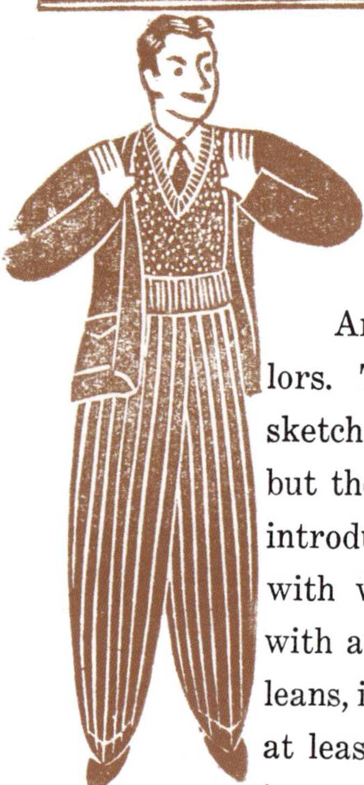

LAST-WORDS

And here abruptly we leave you, Bachelors. The job of showing you about has been sketchily done, for which please forgive me; but these brief chapters may have served to introduce you to a side of New Orleans life with which no other publication has dealt with attentively. And that side of New Orleans, its entertainment side, is, for Bachelors, at least, the most interesting if not the most important.

Other books, many of them, deal exhaustively and well with New Orleans in the round, so to speak, and they are recommended to the Bachelor who has the time and energy to read them. Particularly valuable to lovers of New Orleans—and that includes everyone who has ever been here — is the Louisiana Writers' Project's NEW ORLEANS GUIDE, which probably is the most praiseworthy achievement of all the W. P. A. Writers' Project publications.

The author is particularly grateful for suggestions and for assistance in gathering material for this book to many, especially E. P. O'Donnell; Thomas Caplinger, of Cafe Lafitte; Joe Guerera, of the Hotel Senator Bar (the best bartender I know and the man who so kindly showed me in detail what goes on behind the mahogany); and Frances, my wife, who bore with me patiently when I did much research work for the Chapter entitled OF DRINK AND THE DEVIL.

—R. K.

New Orleans
January 1942

FOR THIS EDITION

of

THE BACHELOR

in

NEW ORLEANS

The 12 Point Century
Expanded Type
was Linotyped by
ED. B. COSTE

and

Printed by
LESLIE E. SELLERS

of

BOB RILEY STUDIOS INC.

in

The Vieux Carre
New Orleans